MAN OF GOD

CHARLES F. STANLEY

MAN OF GOD

LEADING YOUR FAMILY BY ALLOWING GOD TO LEAD YOU

David C Cook®
transforming lives together

MAN OF GOD
Published by David C Cook
4050 Lee Vance View
Colorado Springs, CO 80918 U.S.A.

David C Cook Distribution Canada
55 Woodslee Avenue, Paris, Ontario, Canada N3L 3E5

David C Cook U.K., Kingsway Communications
Eastbourne, East Sussex BN23 6NT, England

The graphic circle C logo is a registered trademark of David C Cook.

All Scripture quotations, unless otherwise noted, are taken from the King
James Version of the Bible. (Public Domain.) Scripture quotations marked ESV
are taken from The Holy Bible, English Standard Version® (ESV®), copyright
© 2001 by Crossway, a publishing ministry of Good News Publishers. Used
by permission. All rights reserved. Scripture quotations marked NASB are
taken from the New American Standard Bible®, Copyright © 1960, 1995 by
The Lockman Foundation. Used by permission. (www.Lockman.org.)

LCCN 2013934364
ISBN 978-1-4347-0547-1
eISBN 978-0-7814-0960-5

First edition published by SP Publications in 1977 © Charles F. Stanley.
Study Guide first published by SP Publications in 1977 © Charles F. Stanley.
Second edition published by Victor Books in 1992 © Charles F. Stanley.

The Team: Alex Field, Amy Konyndyk, Nick Lee, Caitlyn Carlson, Karen Athen

Cover Design: Brian Fowler

Printed in the United States of America

3rd Edition 2013

3 4 5 6 7 8 9 10

080513

CONTENTS

One

THE REAL MAN

In the privacy of my pastoral office, I heard the complaint that launched me on this venture to reclaim man's place under God. A female member of my congregation sat before me, single, frustrated, lonely, and teary-eyed. She saw in her future nothing more than protracted emptiness. It was not long before I realized that her idea of a happy future centered on marriage.

After listening to her reasons for feeling that she should marry soon, I asked, "Exactly what type of man are you looking for?"

Without hesitation she exclaimed, "A *total* man."

"Just what is a total man?" I asked. "How would you describe the man you are seeking for a life mate?"

Thirty minutes later she had completed her description—of a breed of a man that does not exist except in some women's imaginations.

7

THE IDEAL MAN

Since that time I have asked many women the question I asked the young woman in my office, only to find their descriptions unsatisfactory. Some women visualize the ideal man as a strong, healthy, well-dressed, good-looking, aggressive, successful, dependable, and responsible businessman. Others picture someone adventurous, exciting, romantic, and possibly artistic. Either way, he is interested in all things and excels in most. He loves only one woman but charms them all. He's an attentive listener and is in touch with his feelings. And most excellent of all, he is a super spiritual leader in his home.

Have you ever seen anyone who answers this description? Take heart, friend. Neither has any woman. Besides, it presents a distorted picture of the truly complete man.

What is a "total" or "real" man? He is one who understands and accepts the responsibility for the development of his mental, emotional, and spiritual capacity and demonstrates this by his maturing attitude and actions in his personal life, his home life, his vocational life, his social life, and his spiritual life. Now read the definition again with yourself in mind and weigh the emphasis on the words *understands*, *accepts the responsibility*, *development*, and *demonstrates*.

Being a complete man does not depend on background, talent, education, skills, or achievement. It has little to do with looks, size, shape, or age. If these qualities were the criteria, most of us would be eliminated. Neither is a real man measured by how quickly he arrives at his goals or worldly measures of success. Rather, he is a man on a journey, in a process, forging an experience. It involves a journey the Father has planned for every man.

This journey, of course, begins with you acknowledging your need for a Savior. Have you done so? Have you asked Jesus to forgive you of your sins and give you eternal life? You cannot be a true man of God without Him. This is because the moment you ask Christ to save you, He removes your sins, restores your relationship with the Father, and gives you the Holy Spirit to help you become all the Lord created you to be.

If you're unsure about your relationship with Jesus, the first step on your journey to becoming a true man of God involves trusting Christ to bridge the gap your sins have created between you and Him. He is willing to forgive and cleanse you, no matter what you've done. All you have to do is ask in faith, and He will save you right now (Rom. 10:9). You can use the following prayer or your own words:

Lord Jesus, I believe You are truly the Son of God. I confess that I have sinned against You in thought, word, and deed. Please forgive all my wrongdoing, and let me live in relationship with You from now on. I receive You as my personal Savior, accepting the work You accomplished once and for all on the cross. Thank You for saving me. Help me to live a life that is pleasing to You. Amen.

To find out what our Maker intended for us, we must go to His revelation, the Word of God. A glimpse there at the Lord's first perfect man will provide a focus for our understanding today.

ADAM'S CREATION

According to Genesis 1:26, the Father created Adam for Himself—
for His own glory, not man's. Scripture says, "God said, 'Let us make
man in our image, after our likeness'" (Gen. 1:26). The Lord could
not have complimented us more than to make us like Himself.
Humanity is the crown of God's creation. We need to recognize,
therefore, that we were made for God and in His likeness (*imago
dei*) so we can understand the reason for our existence.

We fulfill our eternal purpose when our lives honor the Lord
and reflect His glory. What pleases a human father more than to
hear, "That boy looks just like you; he even acts like you"? God takes
pleasure in spiritual sons who reflect His character.

GOD'S COMMANDMENTS TO ADAM

After the Father created Adam, He gave him three commands. First,
Adam was to rule over the fish of the sea, the fowl of the air, and
over all the earth (Gen. 1:26). Adam's domain was the garden of
Eden, a perfect place for a perfect man and his perfect wife.

Second, Adam was to reproduce. God said to be fruitful and
multiply and replenish the earth and subdue it (1:28). Man was to
bring forth children who likewise would glorify the Lord.

The third command the Creator gave to Adam was: "Therefore
shall a man leave his father and his mother, and shall cleave unto his

wife: and they shall be one flesh" (2:24). That is, a man's wife is to be first in his earthly relationships. God has not repealed these commands. Today it is still a man's responsibility to be a good steward of what the Lord has given, to produce children and raise them to honor God, and to be faithful to his wife.

Psychologists generally agree that all of us are products of our homes. Many people think our past traumatic experiences dominate our present condition, but the general atmosphere of our homes has set the direction and pattern of our lives.

As I counsel people in my church study, one of the questions I invariably ask is, "How would you describe your home life when you were growing up?" Seldom, if ever, does the answer center in a single incident, but is rather an outpouring of the feelings they recall about the atmosphere of their homes. Often such words as *critical, negative, loud, insensitive, unloving,* or *indifferent* are mentioned. Every home has its atmosphere, made up of the combined moods and modes of expression of its members. While each family member contributes to the atmosphere, it is certain that the husband and father has the greatest influence—even when it's by default.

ADAM'S COMPOSITION

The Bible says, "The LORD God formed man of the dust of the ground, and breathed into his nostrils the breath of life; and man became a living soul" (Gen. 2:7). The first man was made of dust—dust that is easily blown away. This fact by itself should protect us from overdeveloped male egos.

God also breathed into man the breath of life, and the dust took on eternal dimensions. Out of that handful of earth, the Lord created a living soul—not just mortal flesh and blood, but a life that is also spiritual in its essence.

The first two chapters of Genesis describe man as God made him to be. The Father placed in Adam's dust-core body a soul with the capacity to think, to rule his domain, to love his wife, and to rear his children. He was given emotions so he could recognize, respond to, and share the needs and desires of his companions. He was afforded the ability to discern the requirements of his family and make choices in their best interest. He was provided with a conscience to guide him to a basic understanding of right and wrong. And the Father gave Adam a spirit to keep him properly attuned to his Creator.

God's first man was neither holy nor unholy—he was innocent. Adam's was an untried holiness, and only he and Eve have ever lived in that condition. All people since then have been born with a sin-prone nature. We have to live with this carnal nature daily, but our Savior has provided victory over it. The innocence man lost in the garden of Eden—which made him less than whole—is offered to us in God's perfect Son, Jesus Christ.

A man may have a perfect body, but if his emotions, mind, and will are not under the control of the Holy Spirit he will fail regularly and tragically as the husband, father, and follower God intends him to be. The Lord designed us not only to cope successfully with the material environment but also to relate harmoniously with other living beings. This is why He endowed man with a spirit—so man can communicate with his Creator and receive wisdom for every interaction and situation. Any man whose body, soul, and spirit are not dedicated to God is fatally handicapped, sadly unable to be the adequate husband or father he longs to be. And no amount of money will make up for the absence of the Spirit of God in his life.

ADAM'S CLAIM

Adam had the right—and obligation—to claim total dependence on the Lord: "God said, 'Behold, I have given you every plant yielding seed that is on the face of all the earth, and every tree with seed in its fruit. You shall have them for food. And to every beast of the earth and to every bird of the heavens and to everything that creeps on the earth, everything that has the breath of life, I have given every green plant for food.' And it was so" (Gen. 1:29–30 ESV).

This is God's promise of provision for man. The Lord declared Himself the source of everything the first man would ever need. His habitation was a gift—the utopian garden of Eden. Good blessings were plentiful and varied. Beauty enveloped him. Man was to be totally dependent upon God.

So it is with the new man—even in not-so-idyllic surroundings. The Father intends for us to live in dependence upon Him, looking to Him for every need. And we can instill in our children the truth of Philippians 4:19: "My God shall supply all your need according to his riches in glory by Christ Jesus." What He did for His first man, He will do through Christ despite our polluted environment.

Not only did Adam have the right to claim provision, he had the right to claim guidance for his life. Scripture says, "The LORD God took the man and put him in the garden of Eden to work it and keep it. And the LORD God commanded the man, saying, 'You may surely eat of every tree of the garden, but of the tree of the knowledge of good and evil you shall not eat, for in the day that you eat of it you shall surely die'" (Gen. 2:15–17 ESV).

What kind of home would you have if you looked to God as the source of every provision? If you looked to the Lord for divine direction of your family? If we could see ourselves as channels through whom God will bless our families with divine resources and direction—if we could be the men He created us to be—we would have homes full of harmony, peace, and happiness such as the world has never known. If we could grasp what God intended for Adam in the beginning and know that His desire for us is the same, each of us would be well on his way toward becoming a complete man.

ADAM'S GOD-GIVEN COMPANION

You may think God would not create anything that was incomplete, but He did. After He created Adam, He looked at His flawless man and saw a deficiency, though not a defect. The lack was a woman.

"The LORD God said, 'It is not good that the man should be alone; I will make him a helper fit for him'" (Gen. 2:18 ESV). Adam needed someone with whom he could share all that the Father had placed in and around him. He needed someone to love. Adam was made in the likeness of God with untried innocence, the totality of what man can be, yet there was no other human being with whom he could share his life. So "the rib that the LORD God had taken from the man he made into a woman and brought her to the man" (Gen. 2:22 ESV). Only then did God declare His whole creation "very good" (Gen. 1:31).

Scripture says a wife is a gift from God (Prov. 18:22)—one that is to be received with gratitude and care. If you are single and looking for a wife, be careful that you wait for the one the Father created specifically for you. Some men feel they got someone else's gift, while others do not feel they got a gift at all. God did not intend marriage to be that way—He wants each spouse to be a joyful blessing to the other. A husband should look at his wife as God's gift to complete him, not to "finish him off." The Lord gave Adam a woman to complement him, not to compete with him. Sadly, when spiritual harmony is missing, home life can be a terrible, disruptive battle.

Scripture also says that God gave Adam a woman who was part of himself—she came from his side. It is then no wonder that the apostle Paul said a man should love his wife as he loves his own body. No man ever hated his body, but cares for it, making sure it has all it needs to be healthy (Eph. 5:28–29). The same is true for your marriage. This is why when you said your marriage vows, you promised to have and to hold your wife for better, for worse, until death parts you (if you spoke the traditional pledges). And those promises were made not only before friends but in the presence of God and are registered in the heavenly records.

Your wife is part of you. The physical consummation made the two of you one.

And God intends for you to have the same relationship with your spouse that Adam had with Eve. The first man was a part of his wife, and she a part of him. If you are not willing to live as a part of the woman you married, your attitude needs to change because you *are* part of your wife and responsible to God for her. When separation divides you, both partners suffer; each is torn apart.

God gave you a mind, a will, and a conscience to guide you in making the right decisions. Therefore, you are accountable for your choices. "Incompatibility" between partners is not an acceptable excuse to Him. Sadly, many couples seek divorce on the grounds of this polite expression. What does incompatibility mean? Many say simply, "We just don't like each other." But differences in personality are never valid reasons for tearing asunder what God has joined.

Scripture says, "Therefore shall a man leave his father and his mother, and shall cleave unto his wife: and they shall be one flesh" (Gen. 2:24). God's pattern for His man and His woman is togetherness forever. That means divorce and separation were not the will of God for Adam and his descendants. I say this from experience, and so would many other brokenhearted people who have endured the torment of divorce—it is never a path one wants to take.

In marriage there will be trials that threaten to tear you apart. God's design for marriage is that it be so tightly knit that nothing can pull it apart. I cannot say that firmly enough to people who are still unmarried. Divorce is one of the most tragic experiences in life. So think long and hard in choosing a partner; be sure that you are getting God's gift for your life.

The best description of a man's responsibility for his companion is a four-letter word: *care*. Ask any woman what she wants from her husband above everything else, and she will probably say, "I just want him to care for me."

Care says much that love does not say, because today the word *love* does not have the same meaning it once had. To a wife, care says, "Whatever your needs are, I am interested in them and am going to do my best to honor them." That is what God intended for His first man. When God said, "Cleave unto her," He meant for Adam to separate himself from everyone else, if necessary, but not to separate himself from Eve. A wife is an integral part of her husband.

One hears many differences of opinion concerning the responsibility of husband and wife. Some people say, "I believe marriage is a fifty-fifty partnership." But the Bible says the *man* is responsible for what happens in his home (1 Cor. 11:3). The husband is the head, or leader, of the wife. How is he to lead? With tender, loving care (see Eph. 5:23–25, 28–29).

ADAM'S RESTRICTION

God said to Adam, "Of the tree of the knowledge of good and evil you shall not eat, for in the day that you eat of it you shall surely die" (Gen. 2:17 ESV). God had provided everything that man needed, but there was one thing in the garden man did not need—the tree of the knowledge of good and evil. Amid all the beauty and perfection of Eden, one thing was off limits. We are all familiar with what happened. Satan intruded, Eve ate the forbidden fruit, and man fell to sin (see Gen. 3).

What should this say to fathers? It clearly teaches that some things are off limits. There are some activities and events in which our families must not participate. Our focus must be on activities that exalt the Father and produce godly joy, fruitfulness, and growth.

God wants to protect us from the painful consequences of evil. Some fathers may say, "Well, we have to learn somehow." But the Bible instructs us that as fathers we are responsible to teach our families to obey the Lord and avoid sin.

Even though no family can perfectly avoid suffering and ungodliness, fathers are still responsible to set moral boundaries for their children and be good examples to them.

ADAM'S CONFLICT

Adam and Eve were happily married, the only couple who ever knew "heaven on earth." They lived in a state of innocence and bliss with no such thing as sin. They could do anything they wished, which by their nature also pleased God.

Adam and Eve's family conflict began when a third party, Satan, deceitfully entered the scene. According to Eve's conversation with Satan, Adam had apparently instructed her about the

Lord's command not to eat the fruit of the tree in the midst of the garden (Gen. 2:17). Genesis 3 exposes Satan's strategy: he persistently asked Eve questions that implied God was not telling her the whole truth.

There will always be family conflicts when we doubt the truthfulness of what God has said or question His principles and commands. When one or both partners, or one or more children, are out of harmony with the Lord's will for a family, conflict is inevitable. God's command to Adam was that he rule his domain; disaster struck when Eve ignored her husband's instructions.

The conversation between Adam and Eve following Satan's victory shows how a woman can influence a man. Satan had to *persuade* Eve to disobey God, but Eve made only one simple suggestion—"Have a bite"—to cause Adam's downfall.

Because of their ability to sway their husbands' opinions, wives have a great responsibility. And the woman who uses her influence wrongly will manipulate her husband to her own regret. Women can connive to get their way if they are clever enough, evil enough, or un-Christlike enough, but seldom are they happy with the results of their scheming.

Many wives know exactly how to get what they want. They know how to dress, what to say, what to give, how to act, and where to go to obtain their hearts' desires. But women who misuse the power God has given them will feel Eve's pain. Eve accepted direction from the wrong source, gained the knowledge of evil, and lost the gift of innocence. Her authority was her husband, but she took direction from an Enemy, Satan. As a result, she received the Devil's due—disillusionment and death.

THREE RESULTS OF THE FALL

In every family conflict there is at least one loser. Here both Adam and Eve lost their beautiful, idyllic home: "Therefore the LORD God sent him forth from the garden of Eden to till the ground from whence he was taken. So he drove out the man" (Gen. 3:23–24). The man, created in the image of God and endowed with all the faculties to make his life complete, was exiled from paradise and sentenced to "hard labor" in the thorn-infested world.

Adam and Eve also lost the unity of their family. When harmony, mutual support, and common goals are gone, is anything of real worth left? Nothing in the world is so sweet as a home with constant peace and agreement among its members, and nothing as wretched as a home without harmony, joy, and love.

The third thing lost was Adam's honor as head of his home. He failed God as its responsible and faithful leader, and the dire consequences were hatred and conflict that cost one son his life and another a lifetime of guilt and fear.

Cain and Abel did not grow up in Eden, but rather outside the garden where their father earned a livelihood by the sweat of his brow, plagued by the sin nature he received when he disobeyed God. Unless you and I strive to obey the Lord in our homes, we will create a spiritually poisonous atmosphere that will infect our children with disrespect for authority—both ours and God's. Pay close attention to this principle: we reap what we sow. Our disobedience today may become our children's rebellion tomorrow.

Adam had no problems before he and his wife fell for the Devil's trap. He communed regularly with the Father and enjoyed life in the garden with Eve and the animals. But pain and suffering invaded his home when Adam failed to shield his wife from their Enemy. Disaster followed.

If you trace a problem in your home to its root cause, you will most likely find the trouble emanates from the violation of a spiritual principle. Spiritual weakness makes our homes more vulnerable than any other liability, which is why the head of the home needs the full spiritual armor offered by God (Eph. 6:11–18).

Adam had every advantage as God's first man and could have easily been a model husband and father for all humanity. But he failed to protect his family against evil. If a man is not effective in his family life, he will not be truly successful in any area. But if he thrives in his home life, he manifests the qualities of the total man—the man God intended him to be.

You recall that my version of a real or total man is one who understands and readily accepts the responsibility for the development of his mental, emotional, and spiritual capacities and demonstrates this by his maturing attitude and actions in his personal life, home life, vocational life, social life, and spiritual life.

How is your progress toward real manhood? Wherever you stand, are you ready to move forward? I'm with you!

Two

MAN OF STEEL AND VELVET

Have you ever considered what spiritual heritage you are leaving for your family? What inheritance those who come after you will receive? We know the apostle Paul spent a great deal of time considering this because he expressed his concern to his "true child in the faith," Timothy (1 Tim. 1:2 ESV). Paul wrote,

> My child, be strengthened by the grace that is in Christ Jesus, and what you have heard from me in the presence of many witnesses entrust to faithful men who will be able to teach others also....
>
> Think over what I say, for the Lord will give you understanding in everything.
>
> Remember Jesus Christ, risen from the dead, the offspring of David, as preached in my gospel,

for which I am suffering, bound with chains as a criminal. But the word of God is not bound! Therefore I endure everything for the sake of the elect, that they also may obtain the salvation that is in Christ Jesus with eternal glory. (2 Tim. 2:1–2, 7–10 ESV)

Paul not only hoped Timothy would remember his example but also longed for Timothy to be a model of faithful godliness others could look up to.

All of us want to leave a legacy—to be remembered for something important. And as believers we have the privilege of passing on a treasure that not only impacts this world but will also endure in eternity. This is why as men it is our responsibility to be a positive example to our children and those who look up to us, teaching them to love the Lord and obey authority. Because when we pass on our faith in the Lord Jesus Christ, we give them a spiritual inheritance, which money cannot buy and death cannot take away.

Sadly, we face an uphill battle. As you may have noticed, it is becoming increasingly difficult to pass on Christian faith and morals to the next generation. Not only can we see proof of it on the news, but we can also see it in the empirical evidence.

For example, a 2008 survey by the Barna Group found that 38 percent of eighteen- to twenty-five-year-olds said they had engaged in sex outside of marriage during the past week, 37 percent had lied, 25 percent had gotten intoxicated, 33 percent had viewed pornography, and 12 percent had engaged in acts of retaliation. A survey taken of Baby Boomers—just two generations older—showed comparable statistics of 4 percent, 6 percent, 9 percent, 16 percent, and 5 percent, respectively.[1]

Who is to blame for the breakdown in passing on faith and morals? There are many causes, but I believe we men must accept the lion's share of the blame. Some men who claim to be the head of their homes simply have done a poor job in exhibiting loving, Christ-centered leadership. Many men have rejected God altogether. The inevitable result is that many young people have copied their fathers' bad habits and ignored their fathers' good ones.

THE RESPONSIBLE MAN

We find in both the Old and New Testaments that God charged men with honoring Him by being wise stewards of what He had given. Regretfully, because of the swiftly declining moral standards and shifting cultural roles, many men are not aware that they remain responsible for their families. But if fathers are passive or unavailable, the consequences can be absolutely devastating. Their children can become disobedient and disrespectful. Their wives may become anxious and frustrated, burdened with endless cares—many of which they were never meant to handle. Their finances and daily schedules will often become tangled and chaotic. And their family communications will frequently become stressful and antagonistic, if they exist at all.

Sadly, many wives believe that the only way to avoid or rectify their family's problems is to take charge of them themselves—assuming responsibilities God never intended them to shoulder. However, when they do so, they unwittingly foster other, more serious issues.

Think about it. What can a wife do when her husband no longer shows any interest in decisions that have been removed from his hands? She no longer receives the support or commitment she desires from him and begins to shut down emotionally and physically. On the other hand, what interest can a man have when his spouse demonstrates her self-sufficiency so thoroughly? No longer experiencing the respect and admiration he needs from his wife, the man likewise begins to distance himself from the relationship. As he retreats, she assumes more of the authority and responsibility. All the while, the children are watching.

Sociologist Gibson Winter observed: "Our tendency today is to assume that we can eliminate the authority of husband over wife and yet retain the authority of husband-wife over the children. The Bible is more realistic about marriage than modern man, for the truth is that in disobeying the one hierarchy we destroy the other."[2]

When a business fails, the head of the company is held responsible, not the man on the assembly line. As the head of the home, a husband and father is responsible for its condition, whether good, bad, or indifferent. Husband, you were given the stewardship of your household—how is that project going? All around us are broken homes, fragmented families, and lonely children. In many cases, the cause is men who refused to take responsibility. Is there any indication that you have failed to accept the mantle of authority God has given you?

You may head a well-ordered home. But if not, do not despair. You can still become the head of your home and the husband God intended you to be.

Writer Carl Sandburg described Abraham Lincoln as a man of "steel and velvet."[3] I believe there is no better description of the kind of man God can work through in a mighty way. In fact, I believe this is the kind of husband and father He wants His followers to be—men of courage and compassion, mettle and mercy. Throughout the rest of this chapter, we will explore what this means in a practical way and how it is possible for your life.

THE MAN OF STEEL

Commitment

A man of steel is *committed*. As a husband and father, he is entrusted with three important tasks: to provide for his family; to protect his family from anything destructive to their minds, bodies, and spirits; and to point his family in the direction of the will of God.

When William Booth, the fearless pioneer of the Salvation Army, was asked the secret of his success, he replied: "From the day I got the poor of London on my heart, and a vision of what Jesus Christ could do with the poor of London, I made up my mind that God would have all of William Booth there was."[4]

One may assume that with such an all-consuming calling, Booth's family must have been neglected, but they weren't. In fact, his children followed his footsteps so closely that biographer Edith Deen declared: "No family in recent Christian history has served so diligently the poor and the outcast, the prisoner and the hoodlum, bringing to them the healing ministry of Christ."[5]

Conviction

Second, the man of steel is a man of *conviction*. He stands firm in what he believes is right. He studies the Bible and knows not only *what* he believes but *why* he believes as he does.

One of the serious problems in families is that fathers do not know their faith well enough to teach it to their children. Many will admit that they have done very little Bible study— excusing themselves with, "I never have been much of a student." But what employee, when asked to read a book of instructions, would tell his employer, "Sorry, but I never have been much of a reader"? Lack of desire is not an excuse for ignoring this important responsibility.

This is why Deuteronomy 6:5–6 first says, "You shall love the LORD your God with all your heart and with all your soul and with all your might. And these words that I command you today shall be on your heart" (ESV). Verse 7 then continues, "You shall teach them diligently to your children, and shall talk of them when you sit in your house, and when you walk by the way, and when you lie down, and when you rise" (ESV).

It is important that a man of God first work on his relationship with the Lord before he attempts to teach others. As I often say, our intimacy with God—His highest priority for our lives—determines the impact of our lives. A man of steel understands this—as well as his responsibility to his family—and acts on it. He realizes that a father cannot expect his children to grow up with strong spiritual convictions if they have learned none from him.

Courage

A third quality of the man of steel is *courage*, which is especially important as we strive to live godly lives in a fallen world. It is important for children to learn how to make decisions based on the principles of Scripture rather than preference even when it is difficult. Sadly, many sons and daughters do not have the privilege of observing how a godly father makes choices that honor the Lord.

Andrew Carnegie said, "To be popular is easy; to be right, when right is unpopular, is noble." There are times when a father needs to say to his family, "That is *not* what we are going to do." He must show that obedience to the Lord is necessary even when it is painful or misunderstood by others.

This is what my grandfather taught me. He said, "Charles, whatever you do in life, always obey God. If He tells you to run your head through a brick wall, go forward, expecting Him to make a hole." This has been one of the most valuable principles I have ever learned—one that has brought me great blessing and fulfillment.

The man who refuses to submit to the Lord because of fear has already hurt his family because of the example he has set. On the other hand, what could be more inspiring to a child than a courageous father?

Character

Fourth, the man of steel is a man of *character*. He is a man of integrity and honesty who can be trusted. Those who know him are confident he will do what he says. He is a man of moral purity who keeps himself for one woman and guards his conduct and conversation so he will not lead anyone into temptation. He has a consistent, daily walk with Christ, which is apparent in his daily interactions with others. He is devoted to God, his family, and his church. And he always stands up for what is right, even when it is costly to him.

A man of sterling character is one whose son will say, "I hope I can be that kind of father." His daughter will say, "I hope I marry that kind of man." Why? Because the man of steel is trustworthy, responsible, and respected wherever he goes.

Constructiveness

A man of steel is *constructive*. He tries to build up others, especially the members of his family. He spends time with his wife and children. He encourages his coworkers and is a blessing to his employer and customers. He edifies the believers in his church fellowship wherever he serves. The man of steel understands that he has both a right and a responsibility to contribute to the society, his home, and his church.

Dad, let me ask you: when you come home after a rough workday, do you slam the door and stalk through the house like an Abrams battle tank? Do you realize how destructive that is? Many fathers are devastating their homes with their damaging attitudes, actions, and words.

Regrettably, what a man *fails* to do may cause as much destruction as the negative behaviors he exhibits. A hardheaded, critical, self-centered father who is determined to have everything his way and who takes no time for his children fails to model the loving, sacrificial leadership demonstrated by Jesus. Because of this, his family may grow hard-hearted and bitter toward authority in general. Even worse, by his example, he may turn them away from God.

However, a man who is building up his family members strives to know their needs and meet them. For example, Proverbs 22:6 instructs, "Train up a child in the way he should go: and when he is old, he will not depart from it." This means we must train each child according to his God-given temperament and qualities. All children are different, and they cannot be treated alike. Therefore, the man who is concerned about building up his family makes it his business to know how his children think and why they respond as they do at their various stages of development. He also seeks to understand his wife and how he can edify her. He strives to be a blessing to her and encourage her in her relationship with God. Knowing what makes a family tick takes a lifetime of learning and understanding but is well worth it because of the wonderful rewards it brings.

Confidence

Another important quality is *confidence*. This does not mean cockiness; rather, the man of steel exhibits the faith of Hebrews 11:1: "the assurance of things hoped for, the conviction of things not seen" (ESV). Why? Because "without faith it is impossible to please [the Lord], for whoever would draw near to God must believe that he exists and that he rewards those who seek him" (Heb. 11:6 ESV). Therefore the man of steel is, first of all, confident in God—he trusts that the heavenly Father is his Sovereign King, Provider, Protector, and Guide. He is confident of God's empowerment, presence, and leadership. He is assured that in Christ Jesus he can do anything that God directs him to do. A man of steel knows where he is going and that the Lord will help him get there. He expects each member of his family to find God's will for their lives, according to Romans 8:28: "We know that all things work together for good to them that love God, to them who are the called according to his purpose."

Control

One final fact about the man of steel: his life is *self-controlled*—which is a fruit of the Spirit (Gal. 5:23 ESV) and a necessary trait for obedience to God. Through prayer and time in Scripture, he aligns himself with the Lord's will and ways. He does not allow his emotions to control him; rather, he lives by the principles and promises of the Word—feeling what God would have him feel and yielding his body as a living sacrifice to the Lord.

You and I owe our families a godly father and husband who is as healthy mentally, emotionally, and physically as it is in his power to be. A man of steel is disciplined—taking proactive, positive steps and avoiding sinful behaviors and harmful actions in order to keep himself in the best condition possible. He realizes that his family needs to depend on him; so he is not willing to cause his family suffering by self-indulgence.

At times, the qualities of steel may seem easy for us as men because popular culture teaches us to be strong, determined, and invincible. But being a man of steel is only half the battle. We are also called to be humble, meek, loving, and self-sacrificing like our Savior, Jesus Christ. In other words, we are called to be men of velvet—the other half of the whole man.

THE MAN OF VELVET

Despite the strong qualities of steel, a man who lacks velvet traits is difficult to live with. Steel is not comfortable or caressable; for human relationships we need responsiveness and humility. We must be men who *care*.

Care

How do we show our loved ones we care about them? It is not just by providing an income for the family, a spacious house for them to live in, stylish clothes for them to wear, and the latest electronics for them to play with. Although providing for them is an important way we demonstrate our concern for them, it is not enough. We must also give of ourselves.

Giving yourself says, "I have time for you. You are important to me." Honestly, how many times recently have you taken your wife into your arms while your mind was actually somewhere else? You were not focused on her; rather, you unconsciously made the choice that something else was more deserving of your concentration. We've all done it—perhaps without realizing that it reveals what we really care about.

Our families need to know we care. I have seen underprivileged families who bear sweet spirits of joy and contentment despite their impoverished conditions. Often, the children think their father is number one because they know he truly cares about them. It doesn't matter what his income is or what things he gives his family. They just know that Dad loves them.

Care is a friendly touch, a loving whisper, a word of encouragement, a solicitous telephone call, and time spent together. Genuine care, for which there is no substitute, may be expressed in a myriad of ways.

Consideration

The second quality of a man of velvet is *consideration*. He takes time to find out the needs of others.

In a church where I was a guest minister, a college student came to me and asked if she could talk with me for a few moments. "I have grown up in a home where my father provided everything we needed," she began. "He is a Christian, the head of our household, and a good provider, but he doesn't know how to listen to us. He has all the answers before we even ask the questions. When I ask him for advice I get volcanic spiels on what I ought or ought not to do. All I want my father to do is let me tell him how I feel."

It happened that I was planning to see this girl's father in the near future, so I asked permission to share her feelings with him. She said it would be all right, but she was not sure she could stand the consequences.

When I had the opportunity to ask this man about his daughter, he said that she was doing fine. His exact words were, "She couldn't be better."

"Would you like to bet?" I asked. He wanted to know what I meant.

"We've been friends a long time, so I'll lay it on the line," I said. "Your daughter doesn't feel the way you described at all." And I repeated what she had said to me.

His first reaction was defensive, to which I answered, "Wait a minute. You may think you are right, but your daughter feels that you never hear her or consider her feelings. Whether you do or not is not the issue. The problem is that she doesn't know that you care."

We may be able to list all the good things we have done, but if our wives and children feel we are not considerate of their feelings, then perhaps we are not communicating with them in the right way or are not being sufficiently sensitive to their concerns. Maybe this disheartens you because you think your family already demands too much of you and wish you could find ways to reduce the burdens you carry, rather than taking on more. However, you may be missing the deeper problem altogether.

Family members may be demanding because their most basic needs have not been met. All the while, you are struggling to meet some burdensome requirements that you thought were crucial but are actually not so important in their eyes. For example, you may be working extra hours to save for your toddler's Ivy League college and post-graduate education, but what your little one really needs is her dad's love and presence. A child is not likely to be lonely, aggressive, and unfulfilled if she has had care, love, and consideration. Your interaction with her is imperative—and will eventually set the foundation of success better than an abundant savings account ever could.

One of the surest ways to show your care and consideration is to take a few minutes each night to ask your son or daughter, "How are you doing? Tell me what's been happening today." Then *listen.* Let your children know that you consider their feelings. Develop sensitivity. You know that something is wrong when your wife is not saying anything. The same is true of your children. When your child comes in from school, knocking, shoving, and carrying on before going to his room—he may have flunked a test; nothing has gone right—what is your reaction? Your first instinct may be to scold him, but discipline will not necessarily meet his need. More than likely his day at school was similar to your day at work. Does scolding help you feel better?

We must remember that our children have feelings and real problems. They get upset when they feel they have been mistreated.

To scold them at that time intensifies their anger and feelings of alienation. We should say, "Tell me what happened. Did someone mistreat you? What can I do to help you?" Nothing stabilizes a child so much as knowing that his father cares what happens to him. The man who is velvet in character takes time to listen.

Cooperation

The third trait of a velvet man is that he is *cooperative.* There are times when every member of the family has to do something he or she would rather not do, and cooperation at the top is called for. You are the chief and have the final authority in your family, but it's essential to pay attention to your family members, give due consideration to what they think, and incorporate their ideas into your solutions. Involve them in the decision-making process and yield to your family's wishes when you can. Your wife in particular may have insight that you lack—listen to her. As Proverbs 19:14 reminds us, "A prudent wife is from the LORD" (ESV).

If what your family wants to do violates your principles, then you will need to override the vote. But use the occasion as an opportunity to teach your children how to make choices based on principle rather than preference.

A man's quality of steel does not mean that he is to domineer. The velvet of cooperation balances the steel of authority. No woman wants to snuggle with a rock. She may admire the strength of steel, but she also loves the feel of velvet. A cooperative man is gentle and good-hearted. He makes every effort to live in peace (Rom. 12:18).

A true leader knows that family life cannot be all grit and valor, and he knows when to yield and smile.

If you are so prideful and inflexible that you refuse to bend your will to others, you will miss some of the finest joys of life. Every child likes to wrestle Dad and win occasionally. It makes a child feel as if he or she can take on the world. The cooperative man makes concessions—never against principle, of course, but simply to please those he loves and to instill a sense of importance and worth in them. He understands the difference between cooperation and compromise.

Communication

A man of velvet is a *communicator*. Some men feel they can communicate better with other men on their jobs than with their wives. Perhaps this problem arises from the fact that a man knows the vocabulary of his business but is not practiced in the language of relationships, so he remains quiet.

Many women ask, "What can I do to get my husband to talk?" Though I am sometimes tempted to jokingly reply, "Be quiet for ten minutes," I know what they are saying. Sometimes a man doesn't have anything worth saying, and sometimes he's too weary to talk. But the man of velvet will make the extra effort to keep communication channels open.

Years ago, my son, Andy, taught me a lesson in communication I will never forget. As we rode down the expressway on the way to church one Wednesday night, my son suddenly stopped in the middle of a sentence and said, "Dad, you are not listening." I had to admit he was right. My mind was on something at the church, and my son noticed I was too busy for him. The same is true for you: when you're not paying attention, your loved ones will notice.

Communication is not just talking; it is also concentrated listening. As a man of velvet, you may need to listen to subjects that don't interest you much and confessions you prefer not to hear. However, it is important for your family to know that you can be reached at all times and that you care about what they think. Your family needs your ears to be open and attentive to them. You may not understand everything they tell you, and you may often disagree with them, but the fact that you have a listening heart will make all the difference in the world to them. So if your children have told you, "You are not listening, Dad," recognize that something serious is wrong with how you're interacting with them, and do all you can to communicate effectively with those you love.

Conduct

A man of velvet also *conducts* himself as a gentleman. I have noticed husbands say and do things that are very unbecoming to a gentle-man. Perhaps their attitudes reflect the general lack of courtesy that mars our whole society. When a woman enters a room and no seats are available, many men will not offer their chairs, though that would be the honorable thing to do. Today, many men expect their wives not only to bring in an income and do most of the housework and child care, but also to mow the grass, wash the car, paint the house, and even fix the furnace. If there is no man around the house, or if a woman enjoys mowing the grass, then it's understandable that she does it. But a gentleman looks upon his wife as someone very special and is careful of the burden he obliges her to carry.

I do not believe a man can justify making his wife work harder than he does. When women feel they are forced to perform heavy tasks, they may be willing to do so with their hands but may also be rebelling in their hearts. Your wife may be cutting your grass with a lawn mower and questioning your character in her mind.

Three
....
A GOOD PROVIDER— AND MORE

A typical American husband may acknowledge that he is not necessarily the citizen he ought to be nor the romantic hero his wife would like him to be. But when it comes to what kind of breadwinner he is, a man will usually proclaim that he is a good provider for his family. He will say that he works hard to supply the material needs of his family. But more than likely he has not asked himself the question: "What provision for my family would benefit them the most?"

One Halloween my house was egged by a teenager riding past in an expensive sports car. Having seen the boy in the act and lacking a taste for eggshell omelet, I phoned the police with a description of the car. In a few minutes an officer returned the culprit to my house to make amends. Shortly afterward, the father drove up to collect his wayward son. Immediately the man began to scold his son for the prank and the embarrassment he caused his family. Then he made a statement I will never forget: "Son, I have given you everything you need and most of what you want, and now look at you."

So many fathers have given all they can to their children, only to be left exasperated and perplexed that their financial generosity failed to teach their offspring decency and respect for others. However, there are three areas in which a father needs to be a good provider: material, emotional, and spiritual. Perhaps it would be helpful to examine from where this responsibility originates.

As Adam and Eve faced a new way of life outside the garden, God told Eve that her husband "shall rule over you" (Gen. 3:16 ESV). With Adam's ordained leadership came responsibility: Adam and his male descendants were to answer to God for the care of their wives and children. And it was not to be easy. "By the sweat of your face you shall eat bread," He told Adam (3:19 ESV). That has been God's plan from the beginning.

The responsibility is just as clear for the followers of Jesus. "If anyone does not provide for his relatives, and especially for members of his household," wrote the apostle Paul, "he has denied the faith and is worse than an unbeliever" (1 Tim. 5:8 ESV). Even those who hate God usually accept this basic responsibility, Paul said.

Providing for one's family is not all drudgery and pain, of course. God knows that man needs a challenge to enjoy life and to mature. Adam confronted a world of weeds, thorns, thistles, wild animals, and a varied climate that taxed his strength and ingenuity. The struggle forced Adam to mature as a man. Daily demands ever since have nudged husbands and fathers toward responsible leadership.

MATERIAL PROVISION

One of the material needs we are responsible for providing is food. The problem today is not so much whether we supply enough, but whether we provide the right kind of nourishment, with adequate vitamins and minerals to help our families stay healthy and strong. With products that emphasize quick preparation and appealing taste, consumers often sacrifice their nutritional needs for foods that merely satisfy their cravings. However, we cannot take it for granted that tasty fast foods are adequate to keep us healthy—we know they aren't. In fact, our terrible eating habits have contributed to many health-related problems, such as diabetes, obesity, high blood pressure, cardiovascular diseases, and many more issues. As a man of God, it is important that you not only encourage your family to maintain a healthy diet and receive adequate exercise but also model it yourself.

A second material need is clothing. Your family need not outdress your friends, but neat and decent clothing indicates respect for the body. Adequate shelter is also necessary, as well as a means of transportation in our mobile society.

The total man recognizes and accepts the responsibility of provision. The material need is actually the least of the three essential needs of every family, though many men don't get beyond the first.

EMOTIONAL SECURITY

The second need is in the area of emotional security. Our loved ones need to feel safe, cared for, and worthy of our time. Sadly, all of the financial and material provision in the world cannot make up for the emotional damage that occurs when these are missing.

Security

In surveys concerning family matters, I have asked a number of women this question: "If you could pinpoint the most urgent need that you as a woman require to fulfill your emotional needs, what would you name?" Nearly every woman without hesitation has answered, "Security." You are responsible for providing a sense of *security* not only for your wife but for your children in their emotional lives.

Security does not rest on a big salary, an impressive home, or possessions. Women tell me, "I don't need the best of everything; what I really want is my husband. I want him to share his life with me." Security arises from the feeling that a responsible person cares about us. Security inspires this reaction: "He is interested in what I am interested in. He cares about me. He won't abandon me." Security deepens when a man says sincerely, "I need you to help me in this problem," because he is communicating that he values the person he is asking for assistance.

Nothing substitutes for security in a woman's life. Though her security should stem from her relationship with God, the Lord works through her husband's devotion, trustworthiness, and consistency in profound ways that touch her deeply. The woman who cannot count on her husband's word and actions is hampered in giving herself to him as he would like. Even if she possesses complete material security, suffering emotional insecurity can cause her untold physical and mental stress. Eventually, the relationship breaks down under the strain of mistrust.

Affection

Another emotional need is for love and *affection*. How does a man show love for his family? The easiest way is by a look. Do you remember your courting days? You may have been sitting across a classroom from her, or at a table in a restaurant, and in one glance you transmitted a whole paragraph. If you have not learned to express your affection for your family through a loving glance, you would do well to learn.

When my children were teenagers, they used to sit near the front of the church, facing the chair where I sat, and they invariably caught my eye just before I stood to preach. Nothing gave me a greater feeling of reassurance than the twinkle in their eyes that said to me, *Dad, we are praying for you.* That is love expressed with only a glance.

Love and affection can also be shown by a touch. The touch is an extension of the real you. How often do you hug your children affectionately? How often do you caress your wife in ways that convey affection without demanding more from her?

If a look and a touch are vital, more so are your verbal expressions of affection. How often do you tell the members of your family that you love them, that you think you have the greatest wife and children in the world?

Have you ever met a woman who does not like to be told that she is beautiful? There is not a woman or child who does not brighten up when paid a compliment. As fathers and husbands who are respected as heads of the home, we can give a word of commendation that will encourage and edify our wives and children. In fact, Hebrews 3:13 commands, "Encourage one another day after day, as long as it is still called 'Today,' so that none of you will be hardened by the deceitfulness of sin" (NASB). Love and affection flourish when you reach out—touching, hugging, looking, saying, and giving of yourself to your family.

Understanding

The third area of emotional need is *understanding*. This does not mean that a man must be able to comprehend women completely—no one is asking for the impossible! God made women mysterious, and we love them for it. Rather, understanding means that we are willing to accept our loved ones just as they are, and we are not continually trying to make them something else. We must make the effort to know them, recognize how they react to different situations, empathize with their struggles, appreciate their strengths, respond with compassion to areas of weakness, and listen carefully to what they tell us. Why? Because when they are understood, they will feel loved and accepted.

Every individual is different. There may be something irritating about one of your children—especially as he or she is growing up—but understanding says, "I accept you though you perplex me." When children say, "My parents don't understand me," they really mean, "My parents will not accept me as I am. They've rejected who I am and what I believe." They may also mean, "My parents are too busy to find out what I think and feel." But when you take every opportunity to truly know them, they will feel appreciated and respected—even if you don't always comprehend what they are saying.

We must love our children even when we must voice our disapproval of any immoral actions they may commit. And we must lead them—not push them—to greater intimacy with Christ and obedience to Him. We must also make time not just to hurry through activities with our children but to listen to them. If they prefer to be distracted by electronics or other pursuits, it's our job to shut those down for some period of time each day or each week so they can learn to communicate with us and we can listen to them.

Time

A man provides for the emotional needs of his family by giving them his *time*. Time is a little word that says:

- "I am willing to get involved with you, son."

- "Honey, I am glad to listen to you and hear your heart."

- "I love you so much that I want to be there for you whenever you need me."

- "You are very important to me."

No father can bring home a paycheck large enough to buy his way out of giving time to his wife and children. Your family needs your presence. When you decide to make your work your priority, rather than your family, there are always consequences.

I confess that early on, I was guilty of putting my work first, and I rationalized my choices by saying, "It's because I'm doing it for God." But I also learned that if we neglect our families, the Lord is not impressed with what we are doing for Him. This is because time together builds oneness with each other and gives us opportunities to teach our children about God. Time with our families transfers our character and strength to them. If a father is never at home with his wife and children, how will they receive what the Lord has given them through him?

Pleasure

A father should not overlook his responsibility to provide *pleasant pastimes* for his family—vacations, camping or fishing trips, or whatever recreational activities teach them about the world around them, help them discover their natural and spiritual gifts, and promote healthy emotional growth. To encourage and participate in enjoyable family pursuits and excursions is not only the father's responsibility but also his privilege.

Attentiveness

Another emotional gift is *attentiveness*. This means uninterrupted concentration on what people say as they say it. A man in our church described being focused during his interactions with his wife in this way: "Attentiveness is my standing still long enough to hear what my wife has on her heart and understanding how she needs me to respond."

Many distractions attempt to claim our attention, so we have to work diligently at being attentive. This is extremely important in every area of your life, because if you are so busy that you are unable to focus on a family member who expresses a desire, joy, or need, you may also find it difficult to focus your attention on God. This can be one of our biggest problems in our relationship with the Father and others—we have never learned to be active listeners who respond to what we are told. It is amazing all the blessings we miss when we fail to be attentive.

SPIRITUAL NEEDS

The third main area of provision for which a man of God is responsible is his family's spiritual needs. As men, we must strive be

MAN OF GOD

Christlike fathers and husbands—not perfect, but maturing. Our children do not need a lecture about Jesus Christ so much as an example of His love, grace, wisdom, and holiness that they can look up to.

A good provider will create an atmosphere in which his family is free to talk about spiritual things. In fact, one of a father's greatest accomplishments is to adroitly and pleasantly apply spiritual principles to areas of his children's interests and troubles—talking them through and helping his sons and daughters to understand the truth behind them. In doing so he builds them up and prepares them for the future.

I found that my most effective teaching was often done in the relaxed atmosphere around the dinner table, where my children could present personal problems or relate a school incident involving a friend. Time after time one of them would say: "Dad, I appreciate the principle we discussed the other day. I discovered that it really works." Practical application of a truth drives it deep into your children's seeking, maturing minds.

Provision in the spiritual area includes a responsibility to counsel your loved ones about eternal matters. Can you lead your children to faith in Jesus? Are you prepared to explain their need for salvation and the forgiveness of sins? You might say, "Since I don't read the Bible much or know much theology, I am going to send my wife and children to the preacher." A pastor doesn't mind helping your family—especially in answering the difficult questions of faith. But if you are sending your family to him because you are unwilling to search out solutions on your own, then you are shirking a major responsibility as a believer and as a father (1 Pet. 3:15). If you

50

earnestly desire to provide for your family, then you must make an effort to understand spiritual matters enough to teach them to your children.

Finally, in the spiritual area, you are responsible for leading your family to a Christ-centered church where the teaching issues from the Word of God. If you have to sift through what is preached and say to your family, "Disregard what the pastor says about this and that," you are most likely at the wrong church. Rather, you should be able to discuss what the family has heard and elaborate on it to build each other up. If your church does not edify your family spiritually, pray about attending somewhere else. Your loved ones need the fellowship of Christian families who love God and who will love them as well.

Who is sufficient for all these things? Every man who puts Christ first! God made us with the capacity to provide for our families: *physically* by endowing us with muscles and minds; *emotionally* by enabling us to cope with the worries and the cares of our family members through time and attention; and *spiritually* by encouraging dependence on the living God within our believing hearts. In other words, we can do all things through Christ who strengthens us (Phil. 4:13).

CAUTIONS

So consider: if an adequate provider is a man who provides for the spiritual, emotional, and material needs of his family, would you say that you are a good provider? If you are not a Christian, of course, you cannot possibly provide for your family fully because by definition you cannot meet their spiritual needs; the Holy Spirit must live in you before you do so. Likewise, if you are a Christian but are not walking in the Spirit, you are not truly able to provide fully for your family either—at least, not in the way the Lord would have you to. The total man is growing in his spiritual life, diligent in his vocation, and loving toward his family—thus training up disciples in the family that God has given him. Is this you? It can be. The Father will empower you if you are willing.

Now, here are some cautions to be observed when providing for your family.

Excessive Provision

First is *excessive provision*—giving your family more than is needed or good for them. Jesus said, "If you then, who are evil, know how to give good gifts to your children, how much more will your Father who is in heaven give good things to those who ask him!" (Matt. 7:11 ESV). Under God, we can provide all that our families need, and like the Lord, we should try to meet their additional desires as wisdom dictates. But when material, emotional, and spiritual provision is excessive, it can be truly destructive—smothering individual initiative, the ability to make decisions, and growth. This is why the Father does not give us everything we ask for and why we should not necessarily accommodate every request we receive from our families—because the consequences of doing so can be absolutely devastating.

For example, an overindulgent father may spoil his child, creating an unreasonable attitude of entitlement. The child may expect to automatically get whatever she wants, whenever she wants it. That child will not feel the need to pray and may even become angry at God when she doesn't get her way.

Instead, it is extremely important to teach our children to pray, wait on the Lord, and accept His answers with praise. This helps our children to grow in their faith, appreciate what they have, and recognize God's authority. This is why it is sometimes better for us to deprive our children of some of the things they want, because in doing so we can teach them the importance of patience, prayer, and of trusting the Lord.

An imbalance in provision can disturb the security of any family. Obsession with material things turns our attention away from God. You may wonder, *What is too much?* Only God knows what is best for your family, so seek Him daily to establish good boundaries. Observe your children, know your wife, and make a wise evaluation of the options the Father gives you. Together your family can set goals so that each member has some responsibility for the successful functioning of the home. God, through you, will provide all that is necessary.

Enslavement to Provision

A related problem to avoid is enslavement to provision—you find yourself working day and night to provide for family desires that go far beyond your actual needs. A husband may do this because of the expectations of his wife. A social-climbing wife may want to partake of every luxury her peers enjoy, regardless of whether or not her husband can afford them. A son may threaten rebellion if he doesn't get the phone, clothes, or car he wants. Sadly, a father with a guilt complex may act unwisely when he constantly hears, "Everyone else has one," taking on a second or third job to supply possessions that may ultimately hurt his family emotionally and spiritually.

Pride

A third problem for the provider may be pride. It is easy to tell if you are vulnerable in this area, because you feel an immense amount of pressure when you realize the neighbors have bigger and better possessions than you do. The idea that you must compete materially to prove your worth is always evidence that you have misplaced pride. Jesus counseled: "One's life does not consist in the abundance of his possessions" (Luke 12:15 ESV).

Many men's ulcers, heart problems, and other diseases are not the outcome of too many hours of work, but the consequences of their emotional stress—their endless focus on reaching the top. Regrettably, when a father's health breaks down, the family may become critical rather than being appreciative of what he has done for them. The reason is that they, like he, rate material gains far above spiritual realities. When their flow of provision is threatened, they become more anxious about their lost comforts than concerned about his declining health. Unfortunately, Dad feels helpless and hopeless because his climb to the top has halted and he can no longer earn his worth in their eyes. He can't figure out what to do because his values are so distorted.

Escape from Provision

Another tragic problem is when men try to escape their duty to provide. Every year more than one hundred thousand men walk away from their family responsibilities. These are not just lazy men with no initiative; among them are men who have lost their sense of identity and dignity. Life's trials have beaten them and crushed their hopes. Job loss is often a major factor, as is illness. But somewhere along the line, many of these men questioned their manhood and deemed themselves to be lacking, so they gave up trying to provide for their families altogether. Even worse, many never discovered the wonderful reason God created them or the awesome plan He has for their lives. They are truly to be pitied, even as their sin of irresponsibility is to be condemned.

Friend, if this is where you find yourself today, don't give up hope. You can overcome these feelings of worthlessness through a relationship with God. Your marriage can survive the loss of your job if you will turn to Christ to find your identity and hope. Don't give in to despair over finding work again. Remember, the Lord works on behalf of those who wait for Him (Isa. 64:4). Continue to seek Him, pursue retraining, and turn to your church for help and support.

Four

GOD'S LEADER

The home is more than a house where people eat, sleep, and talk. The Christian home is a little society, an organization, and a part of the spiritual body of Christ. It is far more complex than most people realize.

The average man marries to enjoy himself, not realizing he has taken on an awesome responsibility to lead his wife and his household. He has become the guide of a small social organism that our Lord Jesus calls a family.

Today we see much confusion and frustration in our homes. One reason is that the man who should be the head of the household has never recognized his responsibility as its leader. I hear married men say, "I'm just not a leader." But I believe that if you are not leading, you are not fulfilling your destiny, because God requires leadership from a husband.

Because of this lack of godly, biblical leadership, American families are foundering in frustration, anxiety, and emptiness with vague goals and little sense of direction. Too many children are struggling because they see no real purpose or meaning in their homes.

Another reason for this problem stems from our perceptions of authority. Too often, we hear the challenge: "By whose authority has the husband been placed over the wife?"

This isn't a plot by men to exploit their wives—it is a biblical principle. First Corinthians 11:3 tells us, "Understand that the head of every man is Christ, the head of a wife is her husband, and the head of Christ is God" (ESV). The Lord designed the husband to be the provider and protector of the wife and the family for a reason, and try as we might we cannot improve on His design.

Ephesians 5:22–23 teaches that the husband is to be the head of the wife and the wife is to submit to her husband. Many principles are implied in this passage, but it is important to note that the passage deals with God's announcement that the husband is the leader of the home—whether he wants to be or not. The only question is whether he is *God's* leader.

The family is an organization that functions twenty-four hours of every day, 365 days of every year. It is one of the most unusual structures in the world, and one of the most important. But strange things are happening to this organizational unit.

The average man comes home every workday evening, eats, stares at a screen or runs around doing activities and errands, goes to bed, and gets up the next morning to repeat the same process—often with little conception of the human assets and liabilities he is handling in his family.

CORPORATION PRESIDENT

Man of God, it is important to understand that in your home, you are the president of a corporation with many divisions. Let me list some of them: accommodation, food service, transportation, education, worship, recreation, finance, counseling, medicine, and maintenance (which includes carpentry, plumbing, sanitation, painting, decoration, lawn service, and perhaps animal care). No other organization in the world attempts to operate so many divisions without help! Nor does any other organization have higher standards for harmony, prosperity, and stability. To become a husband and father is an awesome responsibility in the eyes of God.

The Lord's objective when He established the home was to join husband, wife, and children together in a community that would build them up with love and support and help them mature in the faith. In so doing, all of them would grow in their relationships with Jesus Christ. One of God's objectives is for each member to be motivated to pursue his or her maximum potential as His disciple. So if family members are growing, edifying each other, seeking God's face, and learning the spiritual principles of Scripture, they will continuously be conformed to the likeness of Christ (Rom. 8:29). This is the measure of your corporation's success.

The Lord made men and women equal in value and partners in the family corporation, but gave each significantly different family roles. Unfortunately, the wife who says, "I don't like the idea of submitting to my husband" and has a streak of rebellion within her often undermines herself without realizing it. This is because God has placed the responsibility of the home on the husband in order to free the wife to become the total woman He created her to be. If she competes for the same position, authority, function, and responsibility as her husband, she is running counter to the path that leads to reaching her full potential and maximum fulfillment. The Father has much better, much more satisfying dreams for her, even if she cannot imagine them.

However, we cannot blame our wives for this—the responsibility lies squarely on our shoulders. As I explained earlier, many times our wives will try to take control of our families because we've left a leadership vacuum and they feel they have no other choice. As a result, we feel disrespected, and they feel insecure and unloved. But this clearly illuminates the truth that we cannot lead by proxy or delegate away duties that we're called to fulfill. We must understand that if we continue to oppose or ignore the Lord's design, we will hinder His purposes and His objectives for our families.

This is why it is so important for men of God to take up their mantles of responsibility. We cannot resign our posts. We cannot take a leave of absence or early retirement in this organization. Because to do so would mean undermining our families and ensuring the downfall of our households.

OBJECTIONS

I know some husbands may object with the admission, "My wife is more talented and knowledgeable than I am. She has a better cultural background than I do." That may be an accurate observation, but family order is not based on intelligence or talent—it is based on the Lord's decree given for the best interests of both husband and wife. We may not understand it, but we can accept it as the wise direction of our loving God.

Some new husband may be thinking, *I just got married; what kind of responsibility do I have?* The same. "But I don't have any responsibilities," you insist. Yes, you do!

The alarming thing about so many marriages today is the way people hop in and out of them. Obviously, many do not know what they are jumping into, and unexpected storms send them running.

Some time ago I counseled a couple that was having marital problems. The man wanted to divorce his wife. When asked, "Upon what grounds?" he replied, "Well, I just feel that she'd be better off with someone who could better provide the things in life she wants. I'm willing to get out and let somebody else move in." I told him, "The problem with that route is that another man cannot fulfill your responsibility. Under God, you are both obligated and able to meet your wife's needs." Sadly, young people have somehow gotten the idea that marriage is only for pleasure. Marriage has a lot to do with pleasure, but no less with responsibility.

WHAT IT MEANS TO BE THE HEAD

Some of our problems come from misunderstanding what the head of the home is. God did not make the man superior or the woman inferior at the creation. Not one single verse in the Bible suggests that. Conservative Christians are accused of holding women down and refusing to allow them to fulfill their potential. But Bible believers refer critics to Paul's word in Galatians 3:28: "There is neither Jew nor Greek, there is neither bond nor free, there is neither male nor female: for ye are all one in Christ Jesus." This establishes that all Christians are on the same level and have the same value before God.

When the Lord designates the husband as the head of the wife, He does not suggest that the husband is superior, more intellectual, or more capable than she is. Some husbands may promote this interpretation, and some preachers may carelessly imply it, but God's Word does not support it. The question is not who is better or more privileged but who is the leader in the Lord's family organization.

"Why do we need a leader?" some young people object. "Can't both husband and wife be leaders? Aren't we free to make our own choices? Can't we collaborate?"

My answer is: try to name one project requiring careful decisions by a team of people that has been successful without a designated or recognized leader. Of course collaboration and cooperation are necessary and constructive. But all the way from playground competition to political campaigns, wrangling smothers action and destroys unity unless one leader is recognized. Why do we expect the complex enterprise of marriage to be different?

The family has been given a God-ordained structure to achieve its goals. This structure allocates authority, just as in a business venture. The president of a corporation is not necessarily superior to the vice president in ability, but for the good of the organization and all its team members, cooperation is needed, as is direction and vision from the leader.

As we saw previously, 1 Corinthians 11:3 and Ephesians 5:22–24 give us a chain of command that starts with God:

> The head of every man is Christ; and the head of the woman is the man; and the head of Christ is God. (1 Cor. 11:3)

> Wives, submit to your own husbands, as to the Lord.
> For the husband is the head of the wife, even as Christ is the head of the church, his body, and is himself its Savior.
> Now as the church submits to Christ, so also wives should submit in everything to their husbands. (Eph. 5:22–24 ESV)

If we say that the Bible is wrong in placing the man in authority over the woman, then perhaps we also take issue with saying that Christ is the appointed leader of the church and that God the Father is the leader of the Triune Godhead in its functioning. We either believe the Word, or we don't. Yet we see undeniably that the rest of Scripture affirms that the Father heads the Trinity and that Jesus is the Lord of the church. That reality establishes the remainder of God's chain of command as being *Father, Son, man, woman.*

Despite their different roles in the divine hierarchy, the Father and the Son are equal. Jesus declared their equality with these words: "He that hath seen me hath seen the Father" (John 14:9) and "I and my Father are one" (10:30).

When Jesus walked this earth, He was obedient to His Father. We, in the same way, are to be obedient to Christ, and likewise, our wives are to respect how we lead them. From God's wise view—and He is omniscient, or all-knowing—this hierarchy is the best arrangement for mother, father, and children because it is the most conducive to meeting our needs. Of course, the plan does not work as the Lord intended if the husband fails to love his wife as Christ loves the church!

For the husband to be the head of the house does not mean he goes around beating his chest, expecting everybody to mindlessly obey him or become his doormat. Submission in God's terms means cooperation in fulfillment of a master plan and self-expression within godly boundaries. Everyone who lives by the Lord's plan is under someone else's authority; so each person needs to find his or her unique God-given role.

Throughout Scripture we see that the Father's desire is for the wife to submit to her husband out of love and respect for him. We understand this principle better by investigating how the church is to be subject to Christ. Jesus asked His disciples for their obedience, but He also welcomed their questions and honored their feelings. He set a standard of perfection before them, but He assured them of forgiveness and continued love even when they failed.

When Peter challenged what Jesus was saying, our Lord tenderly disciplined and corrected him (Matt. 19:25–30; 26:31–34). At one time Jesus told Peter he spoke like the Devil, but Jesus still treated him as a friend (16:22–23). Jesus always sought willing cooperation instead of imposing His rightful authority on His followers.

Few women want to leave a husband who is a Christlike head of the home, one growing (not perfect) and exercising his responsibility in love. Of course, there are women and men who want to do as they please and have a basic problem of always resisting God. When someone doesn't want to do what pleases the Lord, they generally don't want to please others either—unless, of course, it advances their self-interests. This attitude breeds frustration, anxiety, and insecurity in a wife who is confused about her proper role in the family. However, a true spirit of surrender to the Father enables us to submit to others according to God's plan.

DEADBEAT AND DICTATOR

Sadly, our image of Dad as the authority figure in the family has suffered two serious distortions. One is the man who demands the respect of his family but doesn't want the many responsibilities that accompany his position as leader. He is indifferent or insensitive to the needs of his family and is inclined to shy away from hard decisions. His detached attitude and indecisiveness create insecurity in his wife and children. He doesn't provide for his family as he should because he is too concerned with his own needs and wants—their lives are constantly in flux due to his temporary whims and grand dreams. His family cannot count on him. Because of his example, the children are likely to grow up with the idea that authority involves lots of talk, little action, and no accountability.

The other distortion is the father who rules as a dictator—an autocratic leader who permits no questioning of his decrees. His word is the first and the last. He rules supreme—but not in the hearts and thoughts of his browbeaten family. He boasts about running his family, but everyone knows he only maintains outward conformity. Behind his back, family members are ignoring him just as he ignores their feelings.

A dictatorial father may be a disciplinarian who knows no leniency, who rules by the word of his law, but he cannot claim such authority from God. Jesus Christ was patient, gentle, and loving. God said we are to rule our families as Christ rules the church. Though His measures are firm, He always acts in love. Likewise, when a man is the genuine head of his family, he doesn't have to prove anything to anyone; he is quietly obeying God and enjoying the results.

The man who wants to make all the decisions without discussion or counsel from others misses one of his greatest opportunities for guiding his children to maturity and his wife to contented partnership. This is because when a man invites his family to participate in decision-making, the younger members of the family receive a feeling of self-worth and confidence, essential qualities for becoming responsible and productive adults.

The autocratic father often resists his family's opinions and ideas because deep down he lacks confidence in himself. His poor self-image is threatened by any suggestion of criticism. Someone has shattered his sense of worth, and he blindly extends the destruction to the rest of his family. One can sometimes see the result of this in wives who get nervous when they see their husbands coming. They live in fear and bondage—not knowing what to expect next or how to avoid setting off their husbands' volcanic anger. Let me be clear: this abuse is absolutely unbiblical.

Regrettably, we can see the effects in the lives of the children as well. A father whose son had been expelled from school for a whole quarter asked me if I would have a talk with his boy. Sitting alone with the son, I asked him to think about himself for a moment and then tell me briefly how he would describe himself. He broke a long silence with the dismal label: "A nobody."

The dejected boy continued to discuss his problem, but his first words had immediately revealed his need. His father—an impulsive, quick-tempered, insensitive, dictatorial man—had destroyed the boy's sense of self-worth. Why should that boy want to please his father? Who can stand being treated as a nobody?

As fathers, we have to acknowledge that our children must be recognized as worthy, unique, and valuable people. They must be understood and accepted as they are. While a dictator makes no allowance for individual personality, the Christlike head of the home rejoices in the varied gifts and abilities of his family. He leads his family in becoming a diverse but unified body that helps one another and serves God faithfully.

BUILDING UP THE FAMILY

God has specifically equipped men to build up each member of their families. If you doubt this, recall the promise of Ephesians 2:10 (ESV): "We are his workmanship, created in Christ Jesus for good works, which God prepared beforehand, that we should walk in them." What better work can we do than to teach our families to love and obey the

Lord? Therefore, together, under Christ's leadership and through our faithful example, the family can become everything God wants it to be.

When a wife has the opportunity to live in a happy, secure home under the leadership of a husband who looks to God, she relishes giving herself freely and being an essential part of the family. She embraces her roles and responsibilities, knowing she is becoming the total woman that God wants her to be—a successful, effective woman, fulfilling her desires and making an eternal impact. She respects her husband, understands her personal equality with him, feels secure in her submission to him, and cherishes the joy and hope God's plan and presence continually give her. Fulfilling her God-given role leads her to deeper intimacy with the Father and a stronger faith. The children likewise benefit as they grow up in the nurture and admonition of the Lord.

If you don't like the condition of your home today, you can improve it. But first there must be an understanding of God's design for your household. Simply stated, His design is for the husband to lead his home with Christlike love, wisdom, sacrifice, humility, and firmness—that is the man's part. The wife is to submit to her husband's decisions and exercise all her abilities in coordinated partnership. The husband must not try to force compliance or respect, just as the wife cannot demand her husband's love. Role fulfillment must be voluntary to be real.

Of course, as men of God, we will still make mistakes—we must allow for this and forgive ourselves when it happens. But if we look to Christ and remain open to the help of others, we will learn from our mistakes. That is the process of maturing, and all of us continue in it until we reach heaven.

MANAGEMENT POLICIES

As I said previously, the husband, as chief priest of the home, has a personal mission to meet the needs of his family. Here are ten practical things a godly leader in a home can and should do.

First, he will see himself as the family leader, as God declares.

Second, in consultation with his family, he will determine the policies by which the household operates—how much money can be spent, how late the children can stay out, standards of courtesy and modesty, etc.

Third, the godly leader will assume responsibility for his decisions—or lack of them. He will not blame others for his mistakes.

Fourth, he will delegate authority for carrying out household duties to his wife and the children according to their abilities and needs.

Fifth, the man of God will guide his family in setting individual and family goals, starting where they are in experience and understanding. A family will most likely have financial goals, spiritual goals, material goals, social goals, and personal goals. The godly leader should gather his family together to talk about the importance of each member playing his or her part to help the family reach these goals. He will show each child the importance of planning for the future as well as acting prudently today. Of course, this is a complex project that requires a substantial amount of time and a good deal of flexibility. Consider spending a few days of your next vacation doing this kind of planning, and you'll see the good effects for the rest of your lives.

Sixth, a godly man will teach his children practical principles for everyday living that will accelerate their progress in their Christian walk and spare them grief.

Seventh, he will be accessible to his family. Children often misbehave to gain attention. They need loving and attentive counsel. When the man of the house is too busy to attend to his household, they may despair that he doesn't care.

Eighth, he will forgive mistakes and continue pardoning the offender "until seventy times seven" (Matt. 18:22), as Jesus commanded. However, some judicious adjustments may be in order before the same mistake reaches that total.

Ninth, a responsible leader will lead his family in regular prayer and Bible reading to nurture the spiritual lives of his loved ones. Relate all of your family's concerns to God during this time by approaching the throne of grace together, and teach your children how to listen to the Lord. Be able to explain how your life is better because of your personal, intimate relationship with the Father. And whenever you see God working in a powerful way, tell your family so they can rejoice with you.

Tenth, the complete husband and father must learn to depend more and more on the Holy Spirit for his daily guidance and power. The Spirit was sent for the purpose of helping you, guiding you, empowering you, maturing you, and giving you wisdom. Submission to Him will make the difference between failures and successes, frustrations and fulfillments. And living by the Spirit will help you follow all the nine preceding guidelines even when you forget them.

Using Solomon's famous description of a praiseworthy wife in Proverbs 31 as a guide, Gladys Seashore wrote the following tribute to God's leader in the home:

Who can find a faithful husband, for his price is far above that of a Cadillac or even a Rolls Royce.

The heart of his wife doth safely trust in him whether he is on a business trip, or comes home late from the office.

He tries to do the best for her and his family.

He learns to use the tools of his trade and isn't afraid of a hard day's work.

He is knowledgeable about world affairs and uses this for his family's enrichment.

He rises early in the morning for his devotions and asks for wisdom for his daily tasks.

He considers investments carefully and buys a home, property, or business with an eye toward the future.

He watches his health and gets the sort of exercise he needs in order to stay physically fit.

His work is of good quality even if he has to put in extra hours to make it that way.

He doesn't neglect his home.

He is concerned about social issues and tries to help those who are in need.

He isn't afraid of difficult times because he has learned to trust God and has done what he could to provide for his family.

He nourishes himself and his family both physically and spiritually.

His wife is well-thought-of in their community because he never belittles her.

He has a hobby that is relaxing and worthwhile.

He is strong and honorable and is a happy person, easy to live with.

His conversation is wise and uplifting. In fact, he makes it a rule of his life to speak kindly.

He is interested in all things that concern his family and is not lazy nor indifferent.

His children love him and admire him, and his wife is proud of him and says,

"Many men have succeeded in this world, but you are the best of them all. If I had it to do over again I would still marry you."

Flattery is deceitful, and good looks are only on the surface, but a man who loves and fears God shall be truly praised.

This sort of man deserves to be treated like a king, for his life proves that what he believes is real.[1]

1. Gladys M. Seashore, quoted in *The Evangelical Beacon*, 1977.

Five

TRAINER IN RESIDENCE

Proverbs 22:6 instructs, "Train up a child in the way he should go: and when he is old, he will not depart from it." Parents sometimes use this biblical proverb to ease the pain they feel when their failures in raising their children begin to show. When children begin to rebel, parents clutch at this promise and remind God of all the ways they led their children to honor Him. However, in some families the nagging question remains unanswered for years: "Did we really train our child in the way he should go?"

As agonizing as this dilemma may be, such parents are still far better off than the ones who deliberately avoid their responsibilities either by abandoning their families outright or by becoming so preoccupied with other interests that the children's training is neglected. The absence of the father's instruction and example leaves a void that may take years of experience and many mistakes to overcome.

From the Lord's point of view, the only man who can count on seeing his grown-up children walking in God's way is the man who is attempting to follow the admonition in Proverbs 22:6—*training* his children in godly ways while they are young. This man of God maintains intimate communion with the Father, confident that the Lord will show him the best way to instruct, discipline, and encourage his children.

An obvious meaning of this proverb is that children will continue to hold the thought and behavioral patterns they developed when they were young well into adulthood. But the truth goes deeper than that: we have a promise that the Word of God planted in a child's heart will continue to bear fruit and work powerfully even when the grown individual is free to make his own choices—it will continue to convict the person and draw him to the Father. The verse suggests God's faithfulness to His Word and mercy to His people (Isa. 55:10–11).

Fathers are inclined to think, *My children are not so bad.* Maybe they are not, but what is hidden in their minds and memories? What are their secrets? Will their actions please you as they grow into more and more freedom? And will they please God? We cannot do anything after our children have left home, but we can impart that training while they are home and anticipate that God will keep His promise in their adult years.

Some parents may protest: "I can't believe that. My children were taught what was right in a Christian home, and look at them now. That verse cannot be true." In fact, one Sunday after I had preached a sermon on the home, a musician who had taken part in the service came to talk with me. He said he had provided well for his family and brought them up in the church, but his twenty-year-old daughter was causing heartbreak and misery for the entire family. He claimed to believe the Bible but added, "I don't believe that passage is necessarily true."

I responded that Proverbs 22:6 is true or none of the Bible is true and reliable. The problem is not with God's promise but with our training. Simply because children live in a home where parents are saved, where the essentials of life are provided, where members give money to the church, pray at meals, and read the Bible once in a while, does not mean they are receiving Christian training.

TRAINING, NOT TELLING

When we delve into the problems a father can encounter in his home, it often becomes evident that training is needed. Even the atmosphere of the household can hinder growth rather than foster it. So before renouncing the promise of Proverbs 22:6, let's see what is involved in training children. I want to challenge you with the following twelve positive possibilities for leading children in "the way they should go."

Faith

The first step involves your own *faith* in God's promises. Are you a man who believes that the Lord exists and that He rewards those who earnestly seek Him (Heb. 11:6)?

We have seen throughout history that God is true to His Word. In fact, Joshua 23:14 proclaims, "Not one word has failed of all the good things that the LORD your God promised concerning you. All have come to pass for you; not one of them has failed" (ESV). Because of this we can trust that Proverbs 22:6—as part of His inspired Word—will likewise be fulfilled and come to pass. When we, to the best of our God-given ability, attempt to train our children properly, we can be certain the Father is also going to do His part.

Let's look at the reverse of the promise: if you train up a child in the way he should *not* go, what will happen? A father who is harsh, inconsistent, and selfish at home, though he carries his Bible to church and holds a church office, will produce resentful and rebellious children. By his unrighteous conduct he has trained unrighteous children. The only deliverance for these children is the grace of God and the work of the Holy Spirit through the influence of another Christian's faithfulness.

Frequently I have heard pastors relate sad tales about their children and then add, "… despite all I have taught them." They perhaps didn't realize that telling and teaching are two different things, and a busy pastor can easily forget that training takes time and intensive effort. Failure to teach good things has consequences just as grievous as teaching bad things.

Christlike Example
Second, a father must be a *Christlike example* to his children. Do you want your child to live according to your words or your actions?

Both form your example. Many fathers say, "Here's what I would like you to do," and the child replies, "But Dad, you didn't do it that way." Someone has said, "A child does what his father tells him until he is fifteen years of age, and after that he does what his father does."

All of us have been training our children positively or negatively since we first held them in our arms. We trained them by what we did, how we did it, and what we said. You and your wife are the strongest influences in your child's life unless you forfeit your responsibility and allow someone else to take over that role.

Someone asked a little boy if he was a Christian. He said, "No, I'm not. My daddy's not one, and I'm just like him." That's a child's honest response to a very serious question. Sadly, our negative influence is picked up more quickly than our positive guidance. Boys and girls are going to be like their fathers and mothers. Whatever we want our children to be, they must see it as well as hear it from us.

I learned this the hard way one Sunday evening as my son drove us to church. We were going quite fast, so I mentioned that the speedometer needle had passed the speed limit. "Well," he calmly answered, "we were running a little late, and I've noticed that when you are in a hurry you usually drive about sixty-five." I had taught him a bad lesson without realizing it.

So consider: How are you using your influence? Are you honoring the Lord through your words and actions? Or have you been slack in your responsibility—hoping your child will somehow turn out okay?

If you want your children to pray, teach them to pray by instruction and example. If you want them to read the Bible, you must read it regularly with them and live by it openly—so they can see your decisions and fruit of your obedience to the Father. If you want them to be kind, gentle, and considerate, you must be kind, gentle, and considerate.

Children have their antennas out at all times. This is because a child's innate desire is to win the approval of his parents. He thinks, *If my father does it, he must like it. If I do it, I will be like him, and he will approve of me.* Therefore he copies his parents in his early years. Everything he sees is a lesson in this early stage. This continues in diminishing degree in later years.

Instruction

Third, we fathers must *educate*. In Deuteronomy 6:7, God instructed the nation of Israel to teach His precepts and principles to their children in the morning when they rose, during the day as they went about their usual activities, and in the evening when they sat down at the dinner table. Can you name one principle you have deliberately, determinedly taught your son or daughter in the last thirty days? When did you consciously attempt to teach them a principle about life—whether it be spiritual or pragmatic? We are the God-given, number-one teachers of our children and there are some basic truths and principles that we need to teach orally and systematically. As I said before, if we fail to intentionally teach them godly principles, they will learn from our negative, ungodly behavior. Or worse, they will be influenced by the three adversaries that are always trying to separate them from the Father—the flesh, the world, and the Enemy.

Instruction needs to relate first to spiritual things. Have you taught your children that Jesus loves them and wants to have a relationship with them? Have you taken time to explain the way of salvation to them? Or have you left that to Mom, the preacher, or the Sunday school teacher? You are responsible for teaching your children how to know the Lord and walk with Him. They are counting on you. You can never shift that responsibility to anyone else.

Salvation is just the beginning, of course. They will need to learn how to live the Christian life and how to apply the spiritual truths that come with every significant step in their growth. We need to educate in pragmatic matters—how to handle money, for example. Even if you haven't mastered the subject yet, you know a great deal more than your children through experience, and you can save them costly mistakes in this important area. Likewise, teach your children about sex at an early age. They need to know that it is for producing children and also for pleasure—but that it is a sacred and private experience between married people. Don't let their young friends provide distorted information about this vital part of life.

I realize that your own father may not have taught you these truths. You may have learned them on your own or through a godly mentor. Perhaps deep down, you feel inadequate and are wondering if your involvement in your children's spiritual development won't do more harm than good. But you are responsible for your children, and you can trust God to make you a good example for them.

If not you, then who will teach them about gentleness and kindness, courtesy and good manners? Their mother will teach them a great deal, of course. But our children also need a living example of how a man should treat a woman with dignity and respect. Likewise, they need to see how we honor God by helping people in need and should observe how we study Scripture firsthand. Watching us practice principles such as "work before play," implement tips on concentration, and take notes to aid our memory are absolutely invaluable. We can't assume the schools or our churches are teaching these things.

As I see the frightening things happening in our society, I shudder to think of children's values being formed by the culture. From celebrity stunts to political scandals, people in the media influence our children's lives in powerful ways that are often neither positive nor godly. Are you willing to leave these crucial lessons to others? This is why it is absolutely imperative that we train our children in the truth and protect them by teaching them how to follow God on their own through prayer and Bible study.

Discipling my son and daughter provided some of the most exciting experiences of my life. For a long time I had been caught up in discipling others; then the idea dawned: *Why not disciple my children—who not only love me but count it a privilege to have me all to themselves?* How richly rewarding this deepening relationship has been for the three of us!

Love

The fourth training need is in *love*. Love is active, unselfish consideration for the needs of others. Our children are starving for someone to love them unconditionally. When a child grows up without a father's love, a sense of insecurity follows that child. He or she may become hostile—difficult to live with and often a detriment to society.

Love says, "I am willing to accept a person though I may reject his attitudes, habits, and lifestyle." When I ask young people, "What is the one quality you want your dad to express above everything else?" they say, "I want him to understand me." We cannot fully understand an eight-year-old, a twelve-year-old, or a sixteen-year-old, but a child wants to know that Dad is *trying* to understand him and accepts him lovingly, even while perhaps disapproving of some of his actions or choices.

Sadly, many parents make tragic mistakes in not distinguishing between the individual and what he or she does. They become so frustrated with their child's bad behavior and choices that they give up. They feel they cannot "fix" the problem, so they reject the youngster—hoping that somehow this will shake their offspring into repentance.

However, this is not the strategy found in God's Word. *Agape* love—the selfless, unconditional love mentioned in Scripture—reaches out and accepts a person as he is, not for what he does or how he looks. A father appreciates his son's or daughter's heartaches and problems, frustrations and fads, and all else that comes along because regardless of what happens, he understands that his child has been created by God and in His image.

One day at the beach, my family was sharing a prayer time after breakfast, and my daughter gave me a great insight. We were talking about the qualities of a father and children's attitudes toward their fathers, and she said, "One thing I've learned is that at this age [fourteen] I realize I must accept you as a person, not just as my parent." Imagine that: she saw me as more than her parent, a person with feelings and attitudes as special to me as hers are to her. She continued, "When I look back at some things I've done and said, I think, shame on me—did I do that?" Understanding me was helping her understand herself.

We need to look at both sides of our disagreements: the parents' and the children's. Children are not "just our kids." They have individuality we must respect and enhance.

When was the last time you told your child you love him or her? I know fathers who are too tough to say, "I love you." Such a father also has a hard time telling his wife he loves her. She's supposed to know that, because "I married you, didn't I?"

To be a healthy child and effective adult, love is essential. Some adults can't get along with other people because they grew up in homes where they were not cared for and never learned how to love. One person struggling with this told me, "I never saw my mom and dad kiss each other. I never learned to express love."

Do you realize that God accepts you fully and wholeheartedly? The Bible says you are accepted in Christ, the Beloved (Eph. 1:6). Not by your goodness, but by His grace (Eph. 2:8–9). In fact, because of this, we are to embrace others. Romans 15:7 admonishes, "Accept one another, just as Christ also accepted us to the glory of God" (NASB). The Holy Spirit sheds the very love of Christ in the believer's heart to share with others—including our children.

Discipline

The fifth thing a father must do is *discipline*. He is instructed to "withhold not correction from the child" (Prov. 23:13). Proper discipline is healthy as well as essential for children.

However, there are four mistakes to avoid in correcting children. First, do not expect perfection. As fathers, we may aim at perfection, but we rarely attain it. When your standard demands that your children make straight A's, you may fail your child emotionally even if he succeeds academically. Forced perfectionism breeds hatred, and that is far from inner perfection.

A good-looking high school senior—an average student but an outstanding athlete—broke down as he poured out his heart to me: "I can never please my dad. No matter what I do, he wants to know why I didn't do it better. I'm buried under his expectations. He wants me not only to be successful, but superior. I'm not interested in being superior; I just want to be me." I heard deep bitterness in his accusation: "He is certainly no example of success himself!" The father's heavy hand of discipline was crushing the boy's spirit and destroying his initiative. We must beware of the egotistical error of trying to achieve our personal ambitions through our children.

A second mistake is overcoercion. For example, imagine your child gets up in the morning and you say, "Wear that pair of shoes. Wear these socks. Brush your teeth. Did you wash your ears? Did you wipe your face? Come to breakfast. Sit down. Get up. Be sure you wipe your mouth before you go to school. Is your hair brushed well? Did you get your lunch? Be sure you are out there when the bus comes. Be home on time. When you get home, carry out the trash. The lawn must be …" And on and on. What would happen? Your child would live in a state of anxiety and with constant feelings of ineptness. When we constantly goad children with "Do this, do that," we take away their opportunities to learn how to make decisions for themselves. This leads to the habit of procrastination—they shut down because they are afraid to make choices. In self-defense they also build other destructive coping mechanisms against the barrage—such as resistance to authority figures.

A man once called me who was having a problem on his job because he refused to do what he was told to do. As we talked, I asked if procrastination was a problem with him, and he admitted it was. "I detest anyone telling me what to do," he said. In his growing years someone had made him despise commands, and he still couldn't handle them as an adult. No doubt the parents were not altogether to blame for their son's problem, but they unnecessarily saddled him with a heavy career handicap.

A third misuse of correction is excessive severity in punishment. Children have an innate sense of right and wrong, and they usually know when they deserve discipline. But undue harshness in their sentences produces genuine moral outrage. Continual violation of their sense of justice will foster callousness and an uncontrolled spirit of revenge. This is why many adults steamroll their way through society in unconscious retaliation against their parents and unwittingly apply the same harsh chastisement to their own children. This is also why there is so much child abuse today. This perversion of discipline is passed on from generation to generation—destroying families and worsening as it goes.

A fourth aberration in discipline is withdrawal of love. When you say, "If that's the way you're going to be, don't expect any more help from me," you are cutting emotional ties even if the threat is never carried out. Nobody can stand strong after personal rejection by a parent.

"You're bad." "You won't amount to anything." "Why can't you be like your sister?" These personal attacks are devastating to one's self-image, and they betray utter lovelessness. Such victims find it extremely difficult to relate to people no matter how friendly they may be. I have seen twelve-year-old children with thick walls around their souls because they have been hurt so much by their parents. Love is a powerful force in both its presence and its absence. Always discipline with love.

Assigning Work

Sixth, *assign work* in training your children. Even when your child is five years old, give him a chore and reward him for completion. To do so teaches children to be responsible stewards who value what they have. When a child fails to do his task, he loses his reward.

Our free society was built on a system of fair compensation for competent effort. Likewise, we are taught in Scripture, "Whoever works his land will have plenty of bread, but he who follows worthless pursuits will have plenty of poverty" (Prov. 28:19 ESV)—we have the promise of rewards for faithful service. Some aspects of our society promote the expectation of something for nothing, but as Christians we must teach our children the reality that we reap as we sow.

We must also show our children that while some chores may earn money or some other prize, certain kinds of work should be done as contributions to the family and in service to the kingdom of God. Children with no chores and no incentive to work will find the transition to a laboring world a formidable hurdle.

Communication

The seventh step in your training campaign should be to *establish communication*. Communication means that you and your children hear each other—not only what is said but also what is meant. This is important because people can't interact with each other effectively unless they express themselves clearly and listen with the goal of understanding. Communication is much more than a mere exchange of words.

There are times when our children simply need to articulate their feelings. Although our first instinct may be to help them fix their problem or to give our opinion, simply listening would communicate more loving concern to them than anything we could say. Doing so helps to build a strong basis for mutual trust and helpfulness.

Notice that Proverbs 22:6 says, "Train up a child [not children] in the way he [not they] should go." Children cannot and should not be put in a category, because each one is different. Each child is developing in a unique way and at a different tempo. Have you realized and appreciated this in your own children? Each needs you to respond to him or her in an individual, distinctive way. It is much simpler to gather them in a circle and say the same thing to all—but they all get varying messages because they hear from their own particular perspectives.

Communication implies that we are willing to find out where each child is emotionally, spiritually, and physically and help her advance in God's plan for her life. It also means that we work to make sure our channels of communication are always open.

Self-Esteem

The eighth step is to *encourage self-esteem*. Every person needs a good image of himself or herself—not one based on false pride, but a self-worth founded in understanding who we are in Christ (Eph. 2:10). Nothing builds up self-esteem in a child like the approval, compliments, and encouragement of a father. When a child is not doing as well as you would like, look for the detail you can honestly praise and give suggestions—not criticism—for improvement. This is love in action.

Sometimes we forget that our children have feelings just as we do. To put them down because they have not reached our level of maturity is thoughtless and imprudent. We must realize their level of competence and try to comprehend the root of their failures. Even when they deliberately do wrong, we can build them up rather than tear them down by discussing their reasons and motives and correcting them in a loving manner. And, of course, we should always remember that each person is more important than his or her actions.

I constantly meet people who lack self-esteem, and almost invariably I discover that they never had the approval of their parents. Even when they did the best they could, it was never good enough. So they grew up thinking, *Why try?* If you don't value your child's initiative, creativity, and self-image and consistently put him down—then expect him to put you down when he grows older. However, if you are loving and edifying toward him—always reminding him of who he is in Christ—the fruit is astounding.

During a late evening chat several years ago, I shared with Andy—who was just a teenager at the time—that I was absolutely delighted by his spiritual growth. He replied, "As far back as I can remember, you have been telling me something that has influenced my decisions." I could hardly wait to hear what it was. He continued, "When I have a son, I'm going to tell him the same thing you keep telling me because it encouraged me and helped me to resist temptation. For years you have said, 'Andy, God loves you, and I believe He has something special for you.'" Evidently my son was hearing: "You are somebody; you are loved; you have the potential to affect eternity," and it made all the difference.

The most wonderful part is that when I turned eighty, Andy again reminded me of the influence of this powerful principle. He had written it down as a commitment in his journal, and he had, indeed, instilled this truth in his children's lives. It is such an awesome blessing to be able to say that it has made all the difference to them as well—one for which I am exceedingly grateful to the Father.

Handling Frustration

The next lesson is *handling frustration.* For example, your child flunks a test and comes home from school with failure written all over his face. Do you say, "Not again!" or "That's tough, son, but we won't give up, will we?" Negative comments do not make a child positive. Through example and encouragement, children need to discover that problems need not lead to permanent defeat.

A common mistake we make is being dismissive about our children's problems. Years of change and maturity have made us forget that a problem with a boyfriend or girlfriend can be a heartrending matter to a young person. Dad scoffs, "Puppy love. You'll be fine. Just forget it." But suppose you and your wife went to a counselor with your problems and he said, "Don't fret, read the Bible, pray, and forget it." We should never disregard our children's problems, frustrations, and anxieties as trivial or unworthy because they don't seem as important to us as our own. They are very real and absolutely crucial to our children.

Instead of offering a quick, simplistic solution, we need to help by showing that we care enough to listen and sympathize.

Try putting yourself in their place and ask yourself: "How would I have wanted my father to respond had I done that?" We fathers need to practice the golden rule at home: "Do unto your children as you would have your children do unto you." By understanding their problems and helping them through, we teach our children that we support them, we care about them, and they can triumph regardless of the frustrations they face.

The Adult World

Further on in training, *introduce your children to the struggles adults face.* The world inhabited by grown-ups is wrought with complications, evil, strife, and danger. Rather than shield children from all knowledge of the harmful influences and pitfalls we encounter on a daily basis, we must prepare them for dealing with this real, difficult, and complex world in manageable doses.

For example, during this economic downturn, many households are facing devastating financial problems. If your family is currently experiencing budgetary troubles, share the issues you face with your children. They will love you for being honest with them. They feel important when they can share your burden and talk to the heavenly Father about the need you have. Introduce them to the world that affects you and someday may touch them—such as what it is like to have a job or your responsibilities as a citizen. And lead them in sensing your need for God and prayer.

Children face some choices that parents must not make for them. Teach them at an early age to ask the Lord for guidance, and then stay with them through the struggle as they seek the will of God for their lives. Children who get ready-formed answers from their parents are adrift when they're suddenly on their own. Overprotection inhibits our children's maturing.

Progress Checks

Naturally, a trainer-coach makes *progress checks* on his players. A corporation president uses all kinds of charts to track how his operations are advancing. With a diagram here and a graph there, he can tell you everything that is happening in his business. But he likely goes home and gives only passing thought to his child's progress. How careless can we be?

How do we keep a check on how our children are maturing? Not by reports and data, but by regular communication, concerned inquiries, and keen observation. You can't keep a scorecard, but you can keep in close touch.

Enjoy Them

The last training project I recommend may not sound like a task, but it is: *enjoy your children*. That seems easier than it is because we identify fun and games with enjoyment, but there is much more involved in truly taking delight in who God created your children to be.

When I used to ask my children, "What is it that you dislike about me the most?" they usually answered, "You're too serious." I realized I was too serious because I was preoccupied with other things, and I had to discipline myself to let go of those concerns before I could focus on having fun with my children. Your children deserve your undivided attention. Give it to them.

But another aspect of enjoyment is appreciation, and I cannot truly appreciate my children unless I know them well and respect their individuality. That takes time and sometimes requires a great deal of patience. But it is well worth the effort.

And in time, as you show your children you truly delight in who they are, you will be blessed as well. Why? Because in time you will see your children show more and more admiration for you and the wisdom of your values.

President Theodore Roosevelt was a dedicated family man as well as conscientious statesman. He said:

> [T]he first essential for a man's being a good citizen is his possession of the home virtues of which we think when we call a man by the emphatic adjective of manly. No man can be a good citizen who is not a good husband and a good father, who is not honest in his dealings with other men and women, faithful to his friends and fearless in the presence of his foes, who has not got a sound heart, a sound mind, and a sound body.... [N]o love for and appreciation of beauty in art or literature, no capacity for building up material prosperity can possibly atone for the lack of the great virile virtues.[1]

Six

REAL LOVE

I believe the most misunderstood word in our vocabulary is *love*. The strife in our society and our homes illustrates our lack of understanding of this important word. Television, magazines, and the Internet make it clear that men have counterfeited its true meaning.

I saw this very plainly when a young couple came to me for marriage counseling. The husband-to-be seemed so uneasy that I asked, "Do you really love this girl?"

He answered unhesitatingly, "Sure I do." So I asked him to tell me why he felt he loved her. He replied, "She does something to me. I feel like a man in her presence. She's what I've been looking for. I think she's very attractive. I know my parents will be proud of me for having such a lovely girl as my wife...." On and on he went, not mentioning a single thing that indicated his love *for her*, but only what she did *for him*. That is not love.

"Free love" and "hooking up" are terms associated with engaging in sexual activity with no strings attached. But love is never free.

All love costs somebody something. You're only deluding yourself if you think you can receive the love you desire without involving yourself. Regrettably, our society is so jaded that it does not know what real love is. Today's love songs speak a different language than the hymns of divine love and the old ballads that linked human devotion to sacrifice.

The Bible communicates the message of true love from Genesis to Revelation. This love encompasses both God and mankind, and it recognizes love's various expressions.

In Ephesians 5, Paul talked about the quality, depth, and core of the total man's love for his family. Very bluntly he instructed: "Husbands, love your wives, even as Christ also loved the church, and gave himself for it" (Eph. 5:25). We understand what that means, but the staggering implications cause most men to shrug their shoulders and look for something closer to the realm of possibility. However, let's look at this idea more closely before we settle for less than God's best.

TRUE LOVE

Love is *unconditional, unselfish, tender, strong action, sacrificially reaching out to do what is best for another person.* This is the purest concept of love—the *agape* love of God for His special creation, man.

Part of our confusion over the meaning of love arises from our use of one word for many kinds of love. We can love a passage of

Scripture, song, family member, sport, pet, chocolate candy, or success—and use the same word for all of them. If there were different words for all the kinds of love that we speak of, however, the dictionary would be considerably more complicated.

According to the Bible, love is a deep, meaningful action that God intends as a unifying factor in our lives. By love we are drawn together and united as one in spirit (Col. 3:14).

Have you explained true, unconditional love to your children? They talk about it, but do they know your version—which I hope is God's version? Do you know how to tell them? Have you modeled it for them?

When you say, "Honey, I love you," do you mean "I like the way you look today" or possibly "You did a great job with that task"? Yes, love has different meanings.

COUNTERFEIT LOVE

The healthy man, whose soul has not been numbed by harmful experiences, knows that there is a distinct difference between sex and love. Sex should include love, but often it does not. Many popular songs portray love as being little more than a kind of animal lust—beneath the dignity of people made in the image of God. Far from being love, illicit sex is a sin by which a man "destroyeth his own soul" (Prov. 6:32).

Both single people and married couples are in danger of expressing selfishness, hostility, and contempt through sex. This is because the world has distorted its meaning and purpose, none of which are according to God's plan. The Lord created sex to be the deepest intimacy between committed husband and wife; therefore, its perversion becomes the highest travesty against love.

A woman would like to live her whole life experiencing romantic love, because God made women to be cared for, cherished, and adored. This is why it is so important for a man to keep romance as part of his marriage—your wife needs it! Sex, love, and romance are not always synonymous, but they can be—and they are for the complete man.

Romantic love reaches out in little ways, showing attention and admiration. The romantic husband remembers what pleases his wife, what excites her, and what surprises her. He reminds her often that she is the most special person in his life, because he knows it energizes her.

Someone once said that in infancy a woman needs love and care, in childhood she needs fun, in her twenties she needs romance, in her thirties she needs admiration, in her forties she needs sympathy, and in her fifties she needs cash. I disagree. I believe a healthy, whole woman needs the same in her fifties as she did in her infancy: unconditional love and tender care. This never changes.

One of the best descriptions of the romantic concept is expressed in this song:

> *Blow me a kiss across the room;*
> *Say I look nice when I'm not.*
> *Touch my hair as you pass my chair:*
> *Little things mean a lot.*

Give me your arm as we cross the street;
Call me at six on the dot.
A line a day when you're far away;
Little things mean a lot....

Give me your hand when I've lost the way;
Give me your shoulder to cry on.
Whether the day is bright or gray,
Give me your heart to rely on.

Send me the warmth of a secret smile,
To show me you haven't forgot;
For always and ever, now and forever,
Little things mean a lot.[1]

If you need help in discerning between true love and the world's false, perverted version, ask this question: will it help me become the person God intended me to be? If the answer is no, then it is not true love.

The man who understands what the Father created him to be knows how he should treat his wife and children. He realizes that true love is unconditional and comes from the heart. He also recognizes he must help those he cares for become the people God intended them to be.

Some men give perfume and diamonds to woo a woman; others try dinners and entertainment. There is nothing wrong with giving gifts. However, what a woman truly longs for is self-giving love from a man who is dependable and responsible—someone who cares for her, protects her, and reaches out to her. His love gives without looking for anything in return.

By the time we reach adulthood, many of us have been playing games instead of loving for so long that we don't realize there is a better way.

LOVE GAMES

One of the games people play is *manipulation*. In this charade, one marriage partner connives to get his or her way while pretending that it's all for the other's benefit. This kind of game hurts both participants.

Then there is *bartering*: "You give me that, and I'll do this for you." Sometimes the game becomes a joke, but it has sobering overtones. Bartering in marriage suggests something illegitimate or unworthy is traded, and that kind of exchange often leads both people to aim at winning instead of giving. What began as a test of wits becomes a contest of spite as each partner feels he or she isn't getting enough.

A third game is *conditional love*. "Sure, I love you, but I loved you more when you did most of the household chores." Or, "How can I love a son who doesn't do this simple thing I am asking of him?" Fickle love of this type is more a gamble than a game, and the dice are loaded against you. Most of us knew some pain from conditional love as we grew up, but we learned to steer away from it.

I read about a man who discovered only in his late forties that he had loved his wife and children conditionally. Even his social contacts were conditioned on the basis that something should be done for him. He said that because his love toward others was based on conditions, he never felt worthy of God's forgiveness—he felt he had to earn it. He simply couldn't accept the Father's unmerited grace. He had grown up with parents who gave him everything on a conditional basis: if he was good, obeyed them, and never embarrassed them, they accepted him.

Conditional love separates instead of unites. People need to love each other for who they are, not for what they do, what they promise, or what they give. Unconditional love says, "I love you because *you are you*. No other condition is necessary."

A perverse kind of love game is *dependency*—obligation. We see it most often exhibited by a parent who claims first place in a grown offspring's life—dominating their time and refusing to allow them their independence. Despondency, loss of an inheritance, or even suicide may be threats these parents use to hold their sons or daughters hostage from living normal lives.

How does the Father love you? He is absolutely without game or guile. Rather, "God so loved the world, that he gave his only begotten Son, that whosoever believeth in him should not perish, but have everlasting life" (John 3:16). His love is unconditional, and "neither death, nor life, nor angels, nor principalities, nor powers, nor things present, nor things to come, nor height, nor depth, nor any other creature, shall be able to separate us from the love of God, which is in Christ Jesus our Lord" (Rom. 8:38–39).

That same love can flow from Christians to others because "the love of God is shed abroad in our hearts by the Holy Ghost which is given unto us" (Rom. 5:5).

LOVE PAUPERS

Some people find it very difficult to love. The person with a poor self-image may feel he or she has little love to share. Yet Jesus said, "Love your neighbor as yourself" (Matt. 22:39 ESV), meaning, "Care for your neighbor as you care for yourself." But what does a person do when he hates himself and dislikes who he is as a person? He's in trouble.

Do you have a hard time reaching out emotionally to others? Deep inside, you want to say, "I'd just like to tell you that I love you today," but you don't say it. We may fear expressing our innermost beings because we have been hurt in the past. We learn to be distant to avoid suffering again.

The most loving people in the world should be believers reaching out to each other (John 13:35), but we are often too tormented by past rejection and regrets to do so. Yet God sets us free to love by restoring our wounded souls and allowing His own unconditional love to flow through us. Are we open to this healing?

Another reason people have a hard time loving is because they are driven to excel in a job, sport, or another pastime. Our national spirit of competition and self-reliance propels ambitious men upward with scant attention to secondary matters.

Sometimes an emotionally battered youth will set out to prove his worth by trying to achieve great goals. Success for this love-starved man is measured by his accumulation of visible wealth and honors. He shows affection by bestowing costly gifts on others—and is bewildered when the recipients show only momentary appreciation. He doesn't realize that his family wants his love above everything else; however, someone must teach him how to love.

Many married people are so confused about how to love one another that they despair, seeing separation and divorce as their only option. They may feel some kind of love for one another, but it is not the edifying, godly love that would energize them. Rather, they have only experienced the exhausting, emotional love games that continue to wound them, interspersed with rare, unsatisfying times of sexual intimacy. It is not enough. But God has the solution.

We all would do well to carefully and prayerfully examine our love relationships with family members. Are we playing conditional, bartered, or manipulative love games? How can we start loving openly—in the godly, unconditional way the Father loves us—without fear of being hurt? We need to begin where we are and immerse ourselves deeper and deeper in God's kind of love—which covers a multitude of human frailties.

COMPETITORS FOR LOVE

I hear people complain about competitors for their love. Wives, for example, must often compete with sports. A frequent complaint I hear is that the wife spends Sunday afternoon working hard at chores and child care, while her husband watches a ball game. And Sunday is not the only day. Of course, this is only a symptom, not the real problem. But it is something specific the husband can change to prove that his wife counts more to him than entertainment.

Television or the Internet may also be your wife's competitor. Or perhaps it's a hobby that preoccupies many of your spare hours. Your wife would not say these pastimes are wrong in themselves, but she is hurt by them if she feels they have more of your attention than she does.

Even friends can become rivals to your wife. A man may express more kindness and give more time and attention to his good friends than to his bride. This is deeply painful to her, and no husband should knowingly inflict such wounds.

Are any of these competitors in your household? Could your wife possibly wonder, *What's the use? I'm no competition for your friends, your hobbies, your programs, your job, or for any of the things you seem to love more than you love me?* If you sense that to be a possibility, your next step is clear: you must give rain checks to your wife's competitors and tell her face-to-face, "I'm sorry if some of my activities have crowded you out. I love you. You're more important to me than my _____, and from now on you're first." But be ready to catch her—she might faint! And be sure you mean to keep your promise—it won't be nearly as difficult as you may fear.

CHRISTLIKE LOVE

Would you like to measure how well you are doing with real, godly love? First, ask God to speak to you as you read His Word, and voice your willingness to accept whatever He shows you. Then read 1 Corinthians 13, and where it says, "Love is patient, love is kind" read "*I* am patient, *I* am kind," etc. The Holy Spirit will help you discern whether your statements are true or whether you are not meeting His loving standards. Is there room for improvement? Don't be discouraged—the God of love is your sufficiency.

How did Jesus love the church? First, He identified Himself with the church, giving us the honor of calling us His body. This is why Ephesians 5:28–29 (ESV) tells us, "Husbands should love their wives as their own bodies. He who loves his wife loves himself. For no one ever hated his own flesh, but nourishes and cherishes it, just as Christ does the church." A man who loves his wife gladly identifies himself with her.

Second, the Lord Jesus Christ supplies everything the church needs to stay healthy and strong. Likewise, the husband should provide for his wife, with God's help.

Third, the Lord Jesus Christ safeguards His people, just as a loving husband should protect his wife.

Fourth, Jesus Christ gave Himself to meet the spiritual needs of His bride. Similarly, a faithful husband gives of himself to meet his bride's deep emotional and spiritual needs.

If a man knows how to romance his wife, love her, build her up, and empower her to become the woman God wants her to be, no one benefits more than the husband himself. "Give, and it shall be given unto you," Jesus promised (Luke 6:38). When a man loves his wife properly, she becomes more than he dreamed and far more than he deserves.

Of course, the greatest expression of Christ's unconditional love was His death on the cross for us. This was the epitome of selfless, generous, unlimited, matchless, measureless, sacrificial love. And this is the way Jesus calls you to love your wife. Impossible? We must remember Jesus's other words: "With men this is impossible; but with God all things are possible" (Matt. 19:26).

A man becomes this kind of lover by first falling in love with Jesus Christ, the source of true love (1 John 4:7). Many Christians have been cleansed of their sin through faith in Christ but do not yet know how to live in profound, loving communion with their Savior. Because of this, they have never experienced the life-transforming power of intimacy with Him.

Do you need to give your life wholly to Christ so you can be filled with His love? If so, simply pray:

Lord Jesus, I want to love my wife with my mind, heart, and body, so I can be the leader and lover she needs. Father, I desire to help her reach her full potential—discovering all You created her to be. But Lord, I cannot do so without Your healing, guidance, and power. I offer my body first to You as a living sacrifice, so I may walk in Your perfect will for my life. Thank You for loving us and for teaching me to love her as You love the church. Amen.

Seven

THE OPENHEARTED MAN

Have you heard about the loving husband who cleaned the house every Saturday morning while his wife slept in? For ten years he exerted his labor of love and never mentioned his selfless service. Imagine the husband's consternation when his wife finally exploded: "If you think I'm such a terrible housekeeper, why don't you clean the house every day!"

That story is fictitious, but it may not be too far from some real-life situations. It illustrates the importance of good communication between husband and wife. Industries spend millions of dollars annually to help employees transmit information more effectively, but little is being done to alleviate the problems of miscommunication in the home. This creates terrible difficulties.

In fact, a group of psychologists I talked with traced incompatibility in many areas of home life to a simple but devastating lack of communication.

To talk and listen with understanding is the simplest definition of communication. Listening is not passive. It is concentrated attention with the ears, mind, and heart, with the goal of comprehending what another person is saying. I find it useful to go back to Genesis to get a clear picture of what the Father created communication to be.

God's main purpose for creating mankind was for companionship. In fact, the first problem the Lord solved in the world He created was loneliness. Genesis 2:18 (ESV) reports, "The LORD God said, 'It is not good that the man should be alone; I will make him a helper fit for him.'" He gave Adam a wife to meet the need for constant human companionship. To fulfill this purpose in marriage, communication was an absolutely essential factor. For Adam and Eve to have real, meaningful fellowship, they had to be able to express their deepest feelings to each other. Any breakdown of that communication would disrupt the flow of life.

THE POWER OF WORDS

Throughout Scripture we are reminded of the power of words. In Proverbs 18:21 we read: "Death and life are in the power of the tongue." Our words can build people up or tear them down in ways few things can.

This is why the apostle Paul instructed believers, "Let no unwholesome word proceed from your mouth, but only such a word as is good for edification according to the need of the moment, so that it will give grace to those who hear" (Eph. 4:29 NASB). Because of their tremendous power, words have the ability to shape us into the people we become—we're all products of the things people have said to us throughout our lives. So it is immensely important for us to guard what we say and be sure that what we're communicating edifies our listeners and does not destroy them.

This is especially true for those who are closest to us. Job complained to his friends, "How long will ye vex my soul and break me in pieces with words?" (Job 19:2). I wonder how many husbands and wives have felt like that. Realizing that "no human being can tame the tongue. It is a restless evil, full of deadly poison" (James 3:8 ESV), we need to examine several things.

First, how deep are we going? In personal relationships, it is important to communicate what we are feeling—our personal reactions to the situations we face. Someone has said that communication between husband and wife is an exploration of the depth of each other's feelings, an experience and adventure in each other's emotions. Sadly, most interaction occurs on a shallow level, never reaching the depths of honest sharing that God intended. We react, spouting off the first, most surface words we can grasp instead of stopping, considering the root of our intense emotions and analyzing why we are truly feeling the way we are. Sometimes we are afraid to expose what is bothering us—we don't like to admit that we feel disrespected or that our manhood has been undermined. So we cloak our true feelings with glib words, while the underlying problem remains hidden, only slipping out through our glances, gestures, and posture. Feelings can't be entirely suppressed.

Let's look at the conversation between Eve and Satan in the garden of Eden. The Devil said, "That's not what God said, or if He said it He didn't really mean it. You didn't understand God's words to you" (Gen. 3:4–5, author's paraphrase). The way Satan twisted the Lord's message played a critical role in man's fall and broken relationship with the Father.

MORE THAN WORDS

I saw a cartoon that read: "I know you believe you understand what you think I said, but I'm not sure you realize that what you heard is not what I meant." That sounds like both parties are confused. When you talk to someone, think through the efficacy of what you've said by considering:

- What you think you are saying.

- What you meant to say.

- What you actually said.

- What the other person heard.

- What the other person says about what you communicated.

- What you think the other person said about what you expressed.

When you say something to your wife, you may think she heard it, but her mind was dealing with more than your actual words. Sometimes we say things casually and expect the listener to understand exactly what we meant. We take for granted that what we said, what we meant, and what we felt are understood. Quite frankly, at times it would take a miracle for that to be true! The recipient of the message may understand one thing from our eyes, another from our gestures, and another from our mouth. When the transmission of the information we're attempting to convey is not consistent in all forms, confusion or misunderstanding results.

When you consider some of the misunderstandings you've had with people you've known many years, you realize how difficult good communications are. No doubt you can recall more than one example from just this week.

As an experiment, give a set of simple instructions to your family, then ask them to whisper them back to you one at a time. Much of the "playback" will be inaccurate.

Often the reason for our misunderstanding is that we filter speech through our own feelings and perspectives, which results in a much different meaning than the original. Sometimes we do not hear what is said because we are busy preparing our rebuttal to the incoming message.

This is why two people who are joined together for the rest of their lives have to make clear communication a priority and must work diligently to achieve it. I recommend daily practice and lots of patience. Acquiring these crucial verbal skills takes work but is absolutely worth the effort.

EXPRESSING FEELINGS

Sometimes our problem is our inability to put our feelings into words. A person says, "I know how I feel, but I don't know how to express it." Because of this, many spouses play the cat-and-mouse game. They run from each other verbally and emotionally instead of articulating what they feel as honestly as they know how. Regrettably, failure to communicate widens the emotional distance between husband and wife.

I am convinced that a prominent cause of broken marriages is the suppression of true feelings by one or both spouses. Many estranged couples have never learned to root out, accept, or express the innermost feelings of their hearts. Because they fear hurting their partner or exposing their own personal weaknesses, they submerge their feelings until a crisis forces them to surface. At that point, an explosion of built-up pain, fear, anger, and bitterness generally occurs—and it shatters much more than illusions. The sudden shock of these raw, unfiltered, visceral emotions unnerves everyone, even though the root cause has existed all along.

FIVE CIRCLES OF COMMUNICATION

Let's look at the five levels or circles in which we communicate. The outermost circle of communication, where we feel the safest, is the circle of clichés: "How are you doing? Good to see you. Looking fine. Hope you are feeling well. How's your family?" Although this communicates a certain interest in an individual, it really does not express much. You neither learn anything nor are inspired to feel anything of any depth.

The second circle of communication is repetition of facts. "Did you hear about this?" or, "The news today is pretty grim." It conveys publicly known information about events and may convey mutual interest in certain subjects such as sports or politics.

The third circle invites the listener to draw closer, which is evidenced by your willingness to express your own judgments or ideas: "His statement was very inspirational." "I won't vote for that."

Deeper yet is the frank expression of your feelings: "To be honest, honey, I feel a little hurt." This circle involves trusting others with your general emotions, allowing them to see more of your personhood.

The innermost circle of communication is the highest and most difficult to achieve because it bares the heart fully with no ulterior motives. We trust the listener so implicitly that we are free to think and feel differently than they do. We know we can communicate even the most difficult emotions without fearing a loss of respect.

Many marriages never pass the third circle of communication: they are willing to talk about places, things, and ideas but shrink back from personal involvement. Little contact of spirit with spirit is made.

At times, men may miss the needs of their families because they don't really know how to hear what their loved ones are saying. In many cases our families do not know how to communicate with us either.

Often all we hear are basic facts. For example, if your wife says, "I don't feel well," she may mean, "Honey, take me in your arms and hold me tight." If we receive only facts and don't pay attention to the innermost feelings she is attempting to communicate, we often miss the real message. A strong marriage is built on the knowledge of feelings that are indeed facts.

In the early years of the telephone, wires sometimes got crossed, and people heard someone other than the person they thought they were talking to. Perfectly intelligent people talked nonsense to each other because they were having two different conversations. Frustration, anger, and helplessness erupted. The effects are similar in some husband-wife communications, with the added complication of not recognizing the problem or sensing how to solve it.

Most men instinctively retreat from emotion. We quickly lose our moorings when confronted with a storm of tears. We do not understand how emotional storms arise from the deep springs within our loved ones' hearts, and we have no idea how to calm them.

Emotions carry important meaning—often inexpressible ones. If the unemotional man of God is to live wisely and productively with his mate, he must meet her deepest needs through comprehending and ministering to her emotions. Tears usually are a cry for tenderness, not talk. They signify that discussion and understanding are needed to resolve a problem. The wise man sees tears as an opportunity for him to open his heart and to grow closer to his wife, who just wants him to love her.

I still remember the day I realized, while repeating the marriage vows to a couple, that there are no "ifs" in them whatsoever. "I take thee to be my wedded wife, to have and to hold from this day forward, for better, for worse, for richer, for poorer, in sickness and in health, till death do us part." Marriage is a contract—but also a relationship. It is an emotional as well as a volitional giving of one to the other. Have you fulfilled your emotional commitment to your wife?

HINDRANCES TO COMMUNICATION

Look out for things that hinder communication with your spouse.

Busyness threatens good communication. When the pace of life gets hectic, the most important aspects of your relationship often get trampled. Slow down and take time for her.

Impatience garbles communication, and emotional irritation will always taint what you're trying to say. Therefore, the next time you feel yourself becoming exasperated in a tense situation, take three deep breaths before speaking and consider whether what you're angry about is really more important than your relationship with your spouse. I promise, taking a step back will save you a lot of heartache.

Communication takes our best effort, but *preoccupation* with other goals turns us away from our ultimate objective. People boast about their ability to multitask, but research shows that most of us can do only one thing at a time well. Be sure to give focused, undistracted time to communicating with your wife.

Insensitivity is a problem because it deflects communication, ignoring some of the subtle cues the communicator is sending. On the other hand, a humble, perceptive spirit is capable of observing the nuances of a message and responding in an effective manner. For example, the Holy Spirit indwelling you is a Supreme Communicator and very sensitive to your needs. Romans 8:26 tells us, "The Spirit helps us in our weakness. For we do not know what to pray for as we ought, but the Spirit himself intercedes for us with groanings too deep for words" (ESV). He expresses the murmur of your spirit to the heavenly Father in a way that is most edifying to you and most acceptable to the Lord. With His help, you can communicate what you feel to your wife. Therefore, pray that He will sensitize your spirit to her.

"Safe" subjects may be a hindrance to you. Do you subconsciously avoid areas of conversation that have produced fireworks in the past? These subjects must be cleared up if you are to know and care for each other at the deepest level.

Children, as wonderful as they are, are often an impediment to communication. When I hear parents say, "We've never left our children with a sitter," I want to tell them what they have missed. Even when children are young, they should be put to bed early so that you and your wife can talk alone and learn about each other. You might be surprised at what you find and how doing so deepens your relationship. Every couple should get away regularly to nurture their own fellowship.

A strong streak of *independence* is an obstacle for some couples. A young woman who talked to me about getting married admitted being pridefully independent, which she realized was a problem. Independence implies, "I only need you for certain things; don't try to possess all of me." This reservation seriously impairs the mutual sharing of life that God intended for marriage. Two remain two instead of becoming one.

Hypocrisy is another hindrance. We may call it sophistication, detachment, or indifference, but what it really means is that we refuse to let our real feelings show. It is possible that you have avoided this modern defense mechanism, but most of us find ourselves pretending to be better than we are at times. This easily extends into family life—covering our real selves and feigning to be something we're not out of fear. Though our intentions may be good, the effect is alienating. To be free we need to be completely honest.

If you have not communicated deeply, you may *fear* being rejected by your mate. You fret: "What will she think if I tell her what I really feel?" The Bible says, "Perfect love casts out fear" (1 John 4:18 ESV). A loving relationship cannot develop and mature when a couple is afraid to express what they feel.

If you and your wife trust each other, you can talk about your goals, what pleases you most, and what hurts you most without anxiety. You may proceed slowly in exploring new depths, but keep moving forward. Joy and excitement in your relationship will certainly increase as you know each other in more profoundly intimate ways.

HELPS FOR COMMUNICATION

Fortunately, there are also helps for good communication. These positive steps can help ward off the hindrances.

Speak clearly. This is partly a mechanical matter of enunciation and partly a matter of taking time to ensure that your message is heard. Careful speech shows respect for the other person and takes the listener's perspective into consideration.

Gently seek the listener's comprehension until your message gets through. We men sometimes want to retreat when our conversations become turbulent. But be assured that if you patiently and prayerfully continue to communicate, eventually your efforts will pay off. Strive to understand your wife more than you seek to be understood by her. This outgoing effort will generate big dividends as your wife responds from her heart.

Another action that helps is to *plan times together*—time for praying, talking, and observing each other's interests. Sharing activities can open new insights into your spouse and grow a deeper appreciation for who she is.

For example, few couples discover how praying together can inspire deep, intense closeness. But I believe the highest, most intimate level of communication often comes when two people talk to God together. As you learn to express your fears and desires sincerely to the Lord, you will experience a growing identification with your spouse's concerns. Sometimes we will say things about ourselves in prayer that we would not say with our eyes open. During prayer, your spouse will often receive a new awareness of the great love in your heart, your humility, and your spiritual aspirations. This is because the Father's divine love always draws the praying couple closer to Himself and to each other.

Develop one or more mutual interests. This may require a sacrifice of preferred pastimes, but the resulting companionship will strengthen the sense of oneness and the awareness of how to meet each other's needs. Start small if necessary, but find something you both like and make it a permanent part of your lives.

EMOTIONAL MATURITY

God gave the husband and wife to each other to make them more together than they could be on their own. However, they can't complete each other until they learn to share their innermost being and work for the good of the other. The personal areas that they keep private—from their spouse and from the Father—have no opportunity for growth.

Marriage, love, and communication cannot be pursued apart from the Lord without greatly hindering and even damaging them. There may be many areas of your life that you've marked "off limits" to God as well as to your wife. Could they be due to fear of inadequacy or rejection, deeply rooted unforgiveness or bitterness, or simply a lack of self-respect? These are poisons in the soul that the Lord and your mate can help dispel—if you will allow them.

So examine yourself for a moment; are you courageous enough to look inward to see what is really there? Are you willing to talk to God and your wife about your hidden self?

We men want to be masculine—to appear strong, invulnerable, and worthy of respect and admiration. However, masculinity involves having emotions in the soul as well as muscles in the body. Therefore, in order to be a real, complete man of God, you must be willing to have your emotions exposed, healed, sanctified, and brought to full maturity. And you must allow the Father to develop and strengthen your soul as only He can.

If you have not matured in this part of your being, pride and/or fear may be your foes. Open your heart to your Creator and your mate, and you will see the Enemy retreating. The fullness of emotional development and interrelationships can be yours.

I challenge you to take these steps to deep communication, first privately and then with your spouse. Because if you do, you will get to know the person you married to the very depth of her being as you learn together. And not only will your marriage improve, but your family and your relationships with God and others will also move toward their fullest potential as you speak and live from the heart.

Eight

JESUS'S MAN

The last clause of 1 Corinthians 2:16 expresses an incredible thought: "We have the mind of Christ." In this passage, the apostle Paul explained the attitude of his heart and moved on to speak of the source of his wisdom and knowledge. In essence he said, "Unlike the wise men of this world, our wisdom came not from our experiences or our study but from the Spirit of the living God who indwells us. Through the Holy Spirit, we have been given the mind of the Lord."

Is that possible? Our non-Christian friends consider us very human, and we ourselves are very aware of our limitations. What did Paul mean when he said Christians "have the mind of Christ"?

I have challenged you to courageously open your heart to your wife, and if you are not able to do that, the reason may be that you have not fully opened your heart or spirit to God. Your basic problem is most likely spiritual. Every Christian has "the mind" of Jesus because He lives within us. Sadly, many believers have not fully submitted themselves to Christ, and therefore have not experienced His renewing, life-changing work (Rom. 12:1–2).

The total man is not a perfect man by any means. Rather, he is a maturing man, a striving man, a studying man—but most of all, he is a man who seeks the Father with all his heart, soul, mind, and strength. He has not arrived at his goal but is on his way to becoming the husband his wife is longing for and the father his children need. He is a man on the most exciting journey of his life. He is learning to be a balanced, Christ-centered man—the total man God created him to be.

Perhaps you worry, *I just don't think I can be all these things to my family. I can't live up to the level of loving that you're talking about, no matter how much I want to. And I'm probably not capable of the profound communication you are suggesting—of understanding my family or of giving them all they need.* You may even feel ashamed that you haven't been the father or husband you should be.

Friend, God does not want you to feel shame. He just wants you to *acknowledge* that you are not experiencing all He has for you. Your repentance and desire to improve are important to the Father. He will use them to work in you and make you all you can be.

When you begin to pursue God's will for you as a husband and father, your family will most likely notice and pray for your spiritual growth. It may not be immediate. But eventually, your wife, no doubt, will see your attempts to be thoughtful of her needs, and your children will say, "I believe something is happening to Dad." You will begin to receive encouragement from their words and the changes you see in their lives.

THE SPIRITUAL MAN

Everything we've considered so far in becoming a total man hinges on this basic principle: *the complete man is a spiritual man.* Therefore, I want to give you some important characteristics of the spiritual man.

In 1 Corinthians 2:14 Paul said, "The natural man receiveth not the things of the Spirit of God: for they are foolishness unto him: neither can he know them, because they are spiritually discerned." Many of the themes we have discussed are found in good psychology, but the deeper, spiritual principles are found in Scripture—biblical truths that come from the study of God's interaction with His creation. From there we understand how important our relationship with the Father really is. And how He must guide us if we are to have successful relationships with others.

The apostle Paul said the "natural man" cannot begin to understand God's basic truths. Paul meant that the man who has not been born spiritually—through faith in Christ as Savior—cannot communicate with the Father or understand the things that must be explained by the Holy Spirit because he simply does not have the capacity to do so. God's knowledge and wisdom are foolish to him because they supersede his ability to comprehend them.

THE RIGHT START

This is why I said early on that the first step to real manhood is spiritual rebirth—"You must be born again" (John 3:7 ESV). The most crucial need of every family is a father whose heart is indwelt by Christ.

Why?

Because by nature, you are spiritually dead, for "your iniquities have made a separation between you and your God" (Isa. 59:2 ESV). You cannot recognize who the Lord created you to be for your family—or even what your family needs from you—because you are completely severed from His presence by your transgressions and cannot receive His guidance.

Therefore, you must believe that Jesus went to the cross to die for your sins and that His sacrifice was sufficient to reconcile you to the Father. When you tell Jesus that His death on the cross was sufficient payment for your sins and ask Him to come into your heart to forgive you, cleanse you, and indwell you, He comes into your life at that moment, and your salvation is guaranteed through the indwelling presence of the Holy Spirit (Eph. 1:13–14).

The husband is the head of his home, and when Christ comes into his heart, he is fully equipped be his family's spiritual leader. He has the indwelling Christ to help him become the total man he needs to be.

Friend, if you are without Christ, you have deprived your family of the one thing they need above everything else—spiritual leadership. However, if you're a man of God, then the Lord can make you into everything your family needs—a man who has the wisdom, grace, and power to take care of them physically, emotionally, and spiritually. There is no substitute for a saved husband and father.

LEADER OF THE LEADER

The second need for a spiritual man is to allow God to lead him. Every child needs a father, and every wife needs a husband who gets his daily directions from the Lord. When your family understands that you seek to live in the center of God's will—and you encourage them to do so as well—your decisions will not be challenged so vigorously or so often. Allowing the Lord to lead you builds your family's confidence in you as their spiritual leader, and observing your dependence on the Father will help them to depend on Him as well. There is no finer inheritance you can pass on to your children than to teach them to seek God for everything and obey Him regardless of the consequences. After all, "The fear of the LORD is the beginning of wisdom, and the knowledge of the Holy One is insight" (Prov. 9:10 ESV).

Children can begin at an early age to talk to the Lord about what they should do with their lives and about their future marriage partners. They should form the habit of asking the Father to help them while they are young. They should also learn that decisions based on human reasoning are not adequate for spiritual success—God must lead them if they desire truly fruitful living.

When my children were young I said to them, "We must wait on the Lord," or, "Let us wait on that and pray together." Later I would follow up with them by asking, "Do you feel like God has said anything to you or shown you how to proceed?" At times they would say, "I haven't heard Him say anything." I wouldn't laugh or scold them—as some parents might be tempted to do. I would just say, "That's all right. You may not understand for a while, but God is in the process of teaching you. If you follow me as I follow the Lord, God can transfer that lesson through me to your heart."

Some of the most precious moments in our home were those when we all knelt in prayer together, seeking the Father's mind and direction. It was always exciting to see who would first receive the clear guidance we needed.

Dad, you can give your children everything else in the world, but if you don't give them a father who has accepted Jesus Christ as Savior and allow Him to lead in decisions, attitudes, and actions, you will never become all the man God wants you to be.

THE PAUSE THAT REBUILDS

The third thing necessary for becoming a spiritual man is to have regular private devotions. We can tell our children repeatedly to read the Bible and pray, but the simplest and most effective way to teach them this spiritual principle is by example—leading a devotion time with them. A father cannot leave this to his wife. You may say, "I travel, and I'm seldom at home." Even if you are not at home very often, your family needs you to lead them in seeking the Lord whenever you are with them. When a child sees his father reading the Bible and praying on his knees, the memory will be irrevocably stamped on his impressionable mind.

I want to ask you, Dad: when was the last time your children saw you on your knees with an open Bible, seeking direction from God? That's an unmistakable lesson to a child. To be a spiritual man you must take time to talk to Him and to listen to Him through His Word. The regularity of this meeting, not its length, is the important thing. Even when you're running late, I suggest you pause long enough to get on your knees and tell the Lord, "I am committing this day to You. Late as I am, I am not leaving home without getting on my knees before You and setting my heart to obey You." God will reward your faithfulness.

Over the years I've seen that the homes of fathers who do this are always richly blessed. Why? Because when we are on our knees before Him, God matures us and guides us in taking spiritual steps each day. Even if you can only pause for a prayer of commitment and a memorized Bible verse in the morning, make sure you do so. That will prepare you for the day ahead. Then you can have a longer period of meditation and Bible reading later in the day when you have more time.

Understand that your attitude of mind influences every aspect of your home, which is why you need biblical principles to be the man, the husband, and the father you want to be. When your attention is focused on Bible truths, you are exercising the mind of Christ—His thinking and manner of responding to circumstances. When you think as Jesus does, you will love your wife and children more faithfully. You are also more sensitive to the needs of those around you.

INSIGHT IN ACTION

The fourth essential to becoming a spiritual man is an awareness of the spiritual needs of your family. A spiritual man is able to discern beyond what is surface or visible. When he listens to his children, he not only hears what they say but also discerns how they feel and recognizes when there's more to what they are experiencing than what they're expressing. The Bible says that Jesus confronted people and knew them inside and out. We do not have Christ's mind to that degree, but as we grow in Him, we increasingly develop His sensitivity to others' needs.

A father who is filled with the Spirit of God can readily discern the basic spiritual needs of his family and looks for opportunities to teach them important spiritual principles. He is also responsible for the spiritual progress of his family. When he sees his children drifting, he encourages them and helps them stay anchored to the solid rock of faith. The man of God also recognizes that his family members need a Christ-centered church where they are taught Scripture, have fellowship with the people of God, and learn how to share their faith. The right church is your great helper in building the right kind of home.

Many years ago, I met a family that was attending a very liberal and rather spiritually dead fellowship. They visited our church several Sundays, and I recall being genuinely concerned about their spiritual wellbeing as I talked to them. There were some strong warning signs that all was not right with them. Sadly, the father seemed either unaware of them or unwilling to acknowledge they existed, so I encouraged him to take his family to a Bible-centered church and get involved as soon as possible.

Two years passed before that father took my advice. I can still recall how he and his wife came forward during the invitation that Sunday morning. Tears streaming down their faces, they shared, "Pastor, we finally made the decision to join, but I'm afraid we waited too long." During those two years, both of their teenagers had rebelled—almost wrecking their lives completely.

That kind of procrastination occurs far too often. Sadly, we are often more concerned about the reactions of fellow church members than we are about the needs of our children. Don't allow that to happen to you.

THE SERVING LEADER

The fifth thing to notice about the spiritual man is that he is alert to opportunities for service—especially when it comes to his family. It took me a long time to learn this, but when it finally dawned on me that it was my responsibility to minister to my family, my whole life changed.

A spiritually minded man will always be on the lookout for opportunities to help his family members. Would you like your son to grow up to be the kind of husband who cares for his wife? How is he going to learn? By reading books? No, by watching his dad. A spiritually minded man has the discernment of the Holy Spirit, and he senses opportunities for serving his wife and children that will help them learn more about the Lord and who they are in Christ.

If we're open and seeking His guidance, God will show us how to bless our families and help them grow in the wisdom and admonition of the Lord. It is then our responsibility to submit ourselves to their needs and to see that these needs are being met. Of course, not all opportunities are spiritual—some are quite practical. It may simply be that your daughter needs help with algebra. You may think, *My wife can help her.* However, your assistance in this practical need has spiritual ramifications. Your daughter needs a tender, caring father, because eventually her view of you will impact her attitude toward authority and her understanding of God. Dad, you may not know the first thing about algebra, but it is not how much you know. Rather, it is your willingness to offer your help that lets your child know that she is important to you. And when she is confident that she's significant to you, she will also have confidence that she's valuable to God.

You may ask, "How does this fit in with a wife being submissive to her husband?" If you want to motivate your wife to trust your leadership, serve her by meeting her needs. The Lord will assuredly inspire her to submit to you as you honor Him.

THE AVAILABLE LEADER

The sixth characteristic of this spiritual man is that he is available to share himself with others. Because he is unselfish, he has a desire to give of himself without expecting anything in return. The joy of giving motivates him to pour himself into his family.

When my children were small, I made an effort to have a brief chat and prayer with them before they went to sleep each night. When they became teenagers, those nightly chats often became much longer and more involved. Because of my schedule, I sometimes missed a session, but not if I could help it. There was something very special about being there to listen to and pray with them shortly before they went to sleep. Because these talks were relaxed and confidential, my children often communicated things that other parents might find surprising. However, they shared because my being there consistently every night communicated, *I care. I am interested in you. I love you.*

A pastor friend of mine was one of a family of seven children. His father, a pastor too, was very busy and away from home until late night after night. But no matter how late he came home, he always knelt by the bed of each child to pray. My friend said he could recall lying quietly as though he were asleep many nights and hearing his father whisper a prayer for him. He said his father's presence for those brief moments always served to calm his spirit. Often when he was tempted during the day, a mental picture of his father kneeling by his bed acted as a bulwark against the Enemy's attacks. Is it any wonder that all of those children married happily, and that four of the five sons became pastors?

Sharing ourselves with our families is time wisely invested, sure to bring rich rewards. This is because we reap what we sow, more than we sow, and later than we sow (Gal. 6:7). The principle of sowing and reaping applies to families just as much as it does to farming.

Not only should a father share himself with his family, but he should also learn to share his faith with others. A father sharing with his family how the Lord used him to lead someone to Christ does more to motivate them to share their Christian testimonies than all the study courses combined.

By demonstration and by instruction we should also teach our children as early as possible to give offerings in the church—not just to meet a church budget, but as an act of love for God in obedience to His Word. Money is an essential factor in everyone's life; therefore, the way to handle money is an important lesson for children. Father, that responsibility and opportunity belong to you. When you tithe, you are investing wisely in the financial and spiritual welfare of your family. And when you experience times of financial difficulty, you can show your children that the strength to persevere and to work through it comes from honoring God in our use of money. These are lessons they will never forget.

Learning to give to God can become an exciting family affair. When you recognize a need, pray about what the Father would have you give, and then respond in obedience together, it can be a very joyful and spiritually powerful experience. These lessons, well taught, will provide a lifetime of financial and spiritual guidance for your children.

THE SPIRITUAL GUARDIAN

The last thing I want to note about a spiritual man is that he abhors everything that threatens the welfare of his family. He will be cautious about the type of television programs his children watch. He will not approve of literature or Internet sites with questionable content nor jokes that imply unkindness or impurity. He is aware that whatever enters the mind remains there—so he is careful in choosing what the children can watch and what activities they can engage in. He realizes that if he doesn't protect his family from the destructive forces of society, no one will.

At times a spiritual man may seem too strict, but he will try to keep a good balance. He lovingly corrects the attitudes and habits that disrupt the harmony of the home. He will not act as a policeman, spying on every activity and telephone call. But as a caring father, he is actively involved because he desires the best for his family.

No doubt you question how any man can live up to all these responsibilities. By himself he cannot, and since no one is perfect, the goal always remains ahead of us. But the possibilities are far greater than most of us imagine—when we take the right steps.

Do you truly desire to be the husband your wife needs? Do you really want to be the father your children long for? I believe you do if you have read this far.

So where do you begin?

Right where you are. If you have never received Jesus Christ into your heart through repentance and faith, you begin there. Romans 10:9–10 says, "If you confess with your mouth that Jesus is Lord and believe in your heart that God raised him from the dead, you will be saved. For with the heart one believes and is justified, and with the mouth one confesses and is saved" (ESV). The first step to becoming the total man—the loving husband and caring father—that your family needs is to ask Jesus Christ into your life as Savior and Lord. The moment you do that, the Holy Spirit will come into your life to abide there forever as your Guide, Teacher, Comforter, and Power. Read John 14 through 16 for Jesus's illumination on this.

God has promised to be your constant Helper as a husband and a father—have you trusted Him for that? Are you daily reading your Bible, praying, and obeying what God shows you to do? You will not build spiritual muscles without feeding your soul and exercising your spirit. Begin there if that's where you are. Ask the Lord for a spiritual partner—your wife or a Christian friend—if you need encouragement to walk in God's path. Seek, ask, and knock persistently, and the Father will open the doors to spiritual power and success.

I challenge you, husband, take one spiritual step toward God today, and He will clearly mark your next step to true manhood and godly leadership in your family.

STUDY GUIDE

An Eight-Session Group Leader's Guide

GENERAL PREPARATION

Survey the entire text of both the preceding chapters and this study guide. Underline important passages in the text and make notes as you read. Become familiar with the entire study before you begin. A general knowledge of what is coming up later will enable you to conduct each session more effectively and to keep discussion relevant to the subject at hand. If a group member asks a question that will be considered later in the book, postpone discussion until that time.

Keep in mind that the outline for each session assumes that group members are reading *the applicable chapter* before each class or group meets.

Add to your teaching notes any material and ideas you think important to your group. As leader, your enthusiasm for the subject and your personal interest in those you lead can determine the interest and response of your group.

We recommend that you plan to use some kind of visual aid, even if you merely jot down answers to group questions on a chalkboard, whiteboard, or pad of paper on an easel. This will impress each point on your group. Then make sure *all* the necessary equipment or material is on hand *before* group time.

Encourage group members to bring Bibles or New Testaments to the meetings and use them during the group time.

GETTING STARTED RIGHT

Start on time. This is especially important for the first session for two reasons. First, it will set the pattern for the rest of the course. If you begin the first session late, members will have less reason for being on time to the other sessions. Those who are punctual will be robbed of time, and those who are habitually late will come still later next time. Second, the first session should begin promptly because getting acquainted and introducing the book will shorten your study time as it is.

Begin with prayer by asking the Holy Spirit to open hearts and minds, to give understanding, and to apply the truths that will be studied. The Holy Spirit is the great Teacher. No instruction, however orthodox and carefully presented, can be truly Christian or spiritual without His control.

Involve everyone. The suggested plans for each session provide maximum opportunity for participation for members of your class. This is important because:

1. People are usually more interested if they take part.

2. People remember more of what they discuss together than they do of what they are told by a lecturer.

3. People like to help arrive at conclusions and applications. They are more likely to act on truth if they apply it to themselves than if it is applied to them by someone else.

4. To promote relaxed involvement, you may find it wise to:

a. Ask the group to sit in a circle or semicircle. This arrangement makes group members feel more at home. It will also make discussion easier and more relaxed.

b. Remain seated while you teach (unless the group numbers and/or venue require standing).

c. Be relaxed in your own attitude and manner. Remember that the group is not "yours," but the Lord's, so don't get tense!

d. Use some means to get the group better acquainted, unless everyone already knows one another. At the first meeting or two, each person could wear a large-lettered name tag. Each person might also briefly tell something about himself or herself and perhaps tell what, specifically, he or she expects to get from this study.

ADAPTING THE COURSE

This material is designed for an eight-week discussion group, but it may be readily adapted to different uses. For a twelve-week quarter, some of the chapters (for example: chapters 2, 3, and 6) can be covered in two weeks, and then a week can be allowed for the group to share what they've gained from the study and what they hope to do differently going forward. For a weekend retreat, ask group members to read the book ahead of time, and then plan eight forty-five-minute (or four ninety-minute) discussion times.

Session 1

THE REAL MAN

SESSION GOALS

1. To get acquainted with one another.

2. To discover God's idea of a "total" man.

3. To understand how sin has warped God's ideal for men.

4. To find a way to express appreciation for our loved ones in a concrete way this week.

PREPARATION

1. If at all possible, read the whole book to gain an overview of the issues you'll be exploring, and jot down the main kernels of truth in each chapter. Then study chapter 1.

2. Read Genesis 1:26–3:24 in light of the teaching in chapter 1.

3. Part of this session focuses on the doctrine that we are made in the image of God (*imago dei*)—existing to fellowship with Him and bring Him glory. Put simply, this doctrine teaches that while we are unlike God in many ways, we are like Him in that we too are *persons*. Like God, we have the capacity to love and to be loved and the ability to build, plan, and create. The fact that we're destined to have an everlasting existence also reflects His image. When Adam sinned, the likeness of God in him was not lost. If the image had involved only holiness, that would be true. But long after the fall, God still sees man as bearing His image (see Gen. 9:6; James 3:9). This doctrine helps explain why we're valuable to God. Humanity has been marred, yet we still bear our Creator's likeness.

4. Plan your session time carefully to allow time at the end for attendees to pray for each other. This should be more than a one-minute prayer. If your group is larger than six or eight people, plan to divide into groups of two or three people for prayer. If your group includes women as well as men, it will often be helpful to have men pray with men and women with women, because people tend to be more candid in single-gender prayer circles.

5. Assemble any teaching tools: whiteboard or chalkboard, markers or chalk.

DISCUSSION

1. If group members don't already know each other, ask them to find someone they don't know and share (a) their name and occupation; (b) the name and occupation of their spouse, if they're married; (c) the names and ages of their children, if any; and (d) the most enjoyable experience they have had with their family in the past year.

2. On your whiteboard, write "The Real Man" at the top. Then write these headings over two columns: "The World's Idea" and "God's Idea." Ask the group to brainstorm a list of ways the world

around them envisions a real man. Write those items under the first column. Then ask them to describe God's idea of a real man, based on chapter 1 of the book and Genesis 1:26–3:24. You might want to have various people read aloud Genesis 1:26–31, Genesis 2:1–25, and Genesis 3:1–24. You can pause after each passage and ask them what it shows about God's idea of a real man.

The following are possible ways to complete the sentence. (The list is not exhaustive.)

A real man is one who …

feels valuable because he's created in God's image (Gen. 1:26–27).

reflects God's character (implied in Gen. 1:26–27).

accepts responsibility as steward of the earth (Gen. 1:26–30; 2:15, 19–20).

recognizes God as His Creator (Gen. 2:7).

obeys God's command (Gen. 1:28; 2:16–17, 24).

recognizes his wife as a gift from God (Gen. 2:21–23).

if and when he marries, leaves his parents and cleaves to his wife (Gen. 2:24).

protects his family from evil influences (Gen. 3:1–7).

doesn't doubt God's Word or question His commands (Gen. 3:1–6).

accepts blame for his own failures, unlike Adam (Gen. 3:11–12).

acknowledges the sin nature he inherited from Adam (1 Cor. 15:22).

yields his emotions, mind, and will to the Holy Spirit (Gal. 5:16–25).

has an attitude of dependence on God's provision (Phil. 4:19).

3. Ask group members to examine the two columns on the board and respond to this question: *What are some basic contrasts between the world's view of a real man and the view depicted in Genesis?*

4. Ask, *What positive things does Genesis 1:26–2:25 say about men?*

5. Ask, *Genesis 3 reports man's fall from innocence. Look at 3:6–24. How did Adam's fall affect his relationship with Eve?* The book section under the heading "Three Results of the Fall" may help here.

6. Ask, *How did Adam's fall affect the way he interacted with God? Look at 3:7–12 in particular.* If group members just quote the passage, such as "he realized he was naked," affirm their answer and ask them to put that into their own words. What does it mean to realize that one is naked? Is this simply a discovery of an obvious fact about one's body that any intelligent person would have noticed before?

7. Ask, *How did Adam's fall affect the way he related to his work? Look at 3:17–19.*

8. Ask, *Given this situation we live in, how do you think a man of God goes about seeking restored relationships with his wife and children?*
The distance between husband and wife should decrease as each partner grows closer to the Lord. Harmony in the home depends on

each partner's intimacy with God and loving obedience to Him. A *real* man recognizes this truth and aids his wife's spiritual development as well as nurtures his own relationship with the Lord.

9. Near the end of chapter 1 Dr. Stanley writes, "A real or total man is one who understands and readily accepts the responsibility for the development of his mental, emotional, and spiritual capacities and demonstrates this by his maturing attitude and actions in his personal life, home life, vocational life, social life, and spiritual life." Read this aloud and ask, *What would motivate us to accept this responsibility? What could motivate us to push this responsibility away?*

10. Proverbs 18:22 tells us, "He who finds a wife finds a good thing and obtains favor from the LORD" (ESV). Read this verse and ask, *What are some practical implications of the fact that God calls a wife a good thing for a man? In what specific ways can we express appreciation for our spouses this week?*

11. Spend time in prayer, possibly in groups of two or three people. If your group includes women as well as men, consider having men pray with men and women with women. Ask them to talk with God about the gap they feel between the person they were created to be

and the person they are. Encourage them to pray about how they experience the consequences of the fall in their own lives and to ask God to lead and empower them in seeking restoration. Ask them to pray for each other in this area.

ACTIVITIES BEFORE NEXT SESSION

Ask group members to do the following:

1. Read chapter 2.

2. Notice the way you interact with the people around you, especially your spouse and children. Record some notes about what you notice yourself doing. Don't criticize yourself or pat yourself on the back; just document how you respond to them. Take your notes with you to your next group meeting along with your copy of *Man of God*. You won't have to share your notes with anyone, so you can be completely honest.

3. Look at the way the Bible portrays the apostle Paul as a man of steel and velvet. For example, look at Galatians 1:1–10; Philippians 1:1–18; and 1 Thessalonians 2:1–9.

MAN OF STEEL
AND VELVET

SESSION GOALS

1. To understand how steel qualities and velvet qualities express themselves in a family.

2. To evaluate ourselves in light of the steel qualities and velvet qualities.

3. To begin working on an area lacking in steel related to our leadership in the home.

4. To put energy this week into developing a velvet quality that we have lacked.

PREPARATION

1. Study chapter 2 and compile a master list of steel qualities, including specific characteristics that Dr. Stanley suggests as well as the seven general qualities he mentions.

2. Brainstorm a list of specific, concrete ways a man could apply these qualities in his life. (Psychological research indicates that people change behavior only if they have specific areas of life in mind and concrete steps to take. For example, being a "responsible" man is a general concept. Rather than having group members leave the session saying, "I need to be more responsible," they should be able to leave concentrating on specific things they can do at home to exercise more responsibility. If you come up with some ideas ahead of time, you'll be able to help them if they can't think of specifics on the spot in the meeting.)

3. Likewise, compile a master list of velvet qualities. Be more specific than just the general characteristics Dr. Stanley lists. For example,

within his comments on the man of velvet as a *communicator*, he refers to *concentrated listening*. Also jot down traits that he doesn't directly mention but that his comments suggest to you.

4. Brainstorm a list of specific ways a man could act on these velvet qualities.

5. There are many more questions in this session than you can probably cover in one meeting. They are provided in case you want to take two meetings for this discussion. If you have just one meeting, read through the questions and decide which ones you plan to ask and which ones you will skip.

6. Have 3 x 5 cards or paper, as well as pens, available for your meeting.

7. Optional: if you plan to cover this session in two weeks, you'll have time to look at some Scripture passages that show Paul as a man of steel and a man of velvet. Become familiar with these passages: Galatians 1:1–10; Philippians 1:1–18; and 1 Thessalonians 2:1–9.

DISCUSSION

1. Begin with a word-association game. Write the words *man of steel* on the board, and ask group members to share the first thing that came to mind when they saw these words. Write their responses on the board.

2. Say, *Steel qualities are the ones traditionally called "manly." Some men are drawn to the idea of being like Superman, while others feel overwhelmed at the idea. However, women and children measure men from a different perspective. Yes, they need and admire the strength of steel. Yet they also love the soft feel of velvet. Character qualities that men easily take for granted are extremely important to others in the family. In this session, we'll learn what it means to be a man of steel and a man of velvet. We'll learn to see ourselves though the eyes of our mates and children and explore concrete ways to achieve greater balance.*

3. The chapter begins with a section on "The Responsible Man." If you have time, here are some relevant questions:

- *What are some specific ways a husband and father can act as a responsible man?*

- *What are some irresponsible things a husband and father may do that would hurt his family?*

- *What factors lead a man to become irresponsible?*

- *How does a man's irresponsibility affect his wife and children?*

- *How does a man's irresponsibility affect his perception of himself?*

4. On the board write the heading "Man of Steel." Ask the group to brainstorm a list of steel qualities. They can draw on the qualities Dr. Stanley mentions in the chapter as well as additional ones they think of. To prime the pump, you can start with a couple of qualities on your list. Then let the group list theirs. When the group has run out of ideas, you can add any on your list that you think are essential to include.

5. Select one of the qualities and ask the group for an example of how a man might act on that quality in his family. Do this for two or three qualities that you think will be most helpful to dig into.

6. Ask, *Which steel quality do you think is most lacking among men today? Why?*

7. Ask, *Which quality do you think is hardest to develop? Why?*

8. Optional: look at Paul's steel qualities in Galatians 1:1–10. Have someone read the passage aloud, and ask the group what steel qualities they see Paul showing.

9. Ask group members to examine the ways they have interacted with others during the past week. If they made notes about this, they can look them over. Ask them to look for evidence of steel and areas where they seem to lack the qualities of steel. Encourage them to be totally honest with themselves and to permit the Spirit of God to convict them and expose their needs. Emphasize that no one will be asked to share what they did. Allow for a time of silent prayer in which members can confess any lack of steel.

10. Pass out note cards and pens. Ask group members to write down one thing they want to do in the coming week that will reflect taking

responsibility as a man of steel. They won't have to share what they wrote unless they wish to.

11. On the board write the heading "Man of Velvet." Ask, *What are some specific characteristics of a man of velvet?* When the group has run out of ideas, add any essential qualities you thought of during your preparation.

12. Ask, *Why do men sometimes take these qualities for granted?*

13. Ask, *What are some mistakes to guard against as a man of velvet?*

14. Ask, *Which velvet quality do you think is most lacking in men today, and why?*

15. Select one of the velvet qualities and ask the group for an example of how a man might act on that quality in his family. Do this for two or three qualities that you think will be most helpful to dig into.

16. Optional: look at Paul's velvet qualities in Philippians 1:1–18 and 1 Thessalonians 2:1–9. Have someone read each passage aloud, and ask the group what velvet qualities they see Paul showing.

17. Ask, *If your mate were listing three velvet qualities missing in you, what would those qualities be? You don't have to answer aloud if you don't want to, but take a minute and think. You might want to write some notes.* Pause for about thirty seconds and let the group meditate on the question.

18. Say, *Take a minute and think of one thing you can do this week to develop one of your weaker velvet qualities. Write that down. You can use the same card where you wrote how you want to be a man of steel.*

19. True growth in these areas is impossible without the Holy Spirit. Take time to pray that the Holy Spirit will begin developing the qualities each group member needs in order to meet the needs of his family.

ACTIVITIES BEFORE NEXT SESSION

Ask group members to do the following:

1. Read chapter 3.

2. Take action on expressing the steel quality and the velvet quality you chose in session 2. If it doesn't go perfectly the first time, don't give up. Habits can take time to develop. Ask God for help.

A GOOD PROVIDER— AND MORE

SESSION GOALS

1. To grow in understanding our mates, particularly their emotional and spiritual needs.

2. To correct any abuse, excess, or insufficiency in our material provision for our families.

3. To discover how we can provide for the spiritual needs of our families.

4. To prepare to discuss with our spouses ways to improve spiritual development in the home.

PREPARATION

Study chapter 3.

DISCUSSION

1. Have someone read 1 Timothy 5:8 aloud. Ask the group, *What goes through your mind when you hear this statement?* Get brief responses from as many group members as possible.

2. Ask, *Why would any Christian who doesn't adequately provide for his household be worse than an unbeliever?*

3. A female perspective on the needs of a family can be helpful to men. If you have women in your group, ask them to respond to one or more of the following questions:

- *What provisions are most essential to your family?*

- *What are some emotional needs of children that fathers can best fulfill?*

- *What are the greatest emotional needs of wives? How can a husband become more sensitive to the emotional needs of family members?*

- *Give examples of things a husband can do to meet his wife's emotional needs.*

4. Ask, *How do you figure out how much is enough material provision for your family? Do you measure that by what your parents had, what other people have, or what you want? Or is there some other standard by which to measure?*

5. Ask, *What does it mean to be enslaved to provision, either by others or by one's own pride? How can you tell if you're enslaved?*

6. Ask, *In the realities of our world, what can a man do if he feels pressure to work excessively, either from his employer, his family, or himself?*

7. Ask, *What did your father do to provide for your family's spiritual needs?*

8. Ask someone to read Deuteronomy 6:1–9 aloud. Then ask, *How does this passage describe the family's role in providing for the children's spiritual needs?* Some important insights to highlight are:

> The basis of caring for the spiritual needs of others rests in having our own needs met through a relationship with God. Our own love for the Lord is the key (vv. 1–5).

> We must model the Christian lifestyle we want our children or spouse to adopt—vv. 1–5. Especially note the stress on parents *obeying* God's commands faithfully before attempting to teach them (vv. 1–3).

> The prerequisite for adequately caring for spiritual needs is saturating ourselves with the Word of God (v. 6).

We can instill spiritual truths spontaneously in life situations as well as in formal times of instruction (vv. 7–9).

9. Ask, *Do you think it's unrealistic today to expect families to provide for the children's spiritual needs? Should churches do the job instead? Why or why not?*

10. Ask, *What ideas for providing for your family's spiritual needs did you get from the chapter?* After the group has responded, ask, *What challenges would you face in putting those into practice? How could a family overcome those challenges?*

11. When confronted with the awesome responsibility of providing for the spiritual needs of family members, many men feel uncomfortable or guilty and see only their shortcomings. Remind your group that the adequacy to fulfill God-given tasks comes from the Father, not from within ourselves. The Lord equips us to do what He commands us to do. Scripture passages focusing on God's capacity to enable us include John 15:1–11; 1 Corinthians 1:26–29; 2 Corinthians 4:7; 12:9–10; and Ephesians 3:20. Take time for group members to pray for each other to grow as their family providers materially, emotionally, and spiritually.

12. Ask each person to think through which of these areas of spiritual input is most lacking in their home: involvement in a church community, or conversation about spiritual things at home. (Or if material or emotional provision is the main issue their family needs to address, ask them to identify that.) Encourage everyone to meet with their spouses next week, and in light of this lack, discuss ways to improve the provision for family members. This should be a brainstorming and prayer session in which husband and wife decide how to strengthen the area of weakness. Encourage group members whose spouses aren't Christians to share their needs and concerns with a friend for the purpose of prayer.

ACTIVITIES BEFORE NEXT SESSION

Ask group members to read chapter 4 of the text.

GOD'S LEADER

SESSION GOALS

1. To clarify misconceptions and correct abuses of the man of God's leadership role.

2. To evaluate ourselves in light of the servant style of leadership proposed by Jesus.

PREPARATION

Study chapter 4.

DISCUSSION

1. Before group members arrive, write the following question on the whiteboard or flip chart: *If you died today, how would you want your wife and children to answer this question: what do you remember most about your husband (father)?* When the group has gathered, ask group members to respond.

2. Have someone read 1 Corinthians 11:3 aloud. On your whiteboard or flip chart, draw a diagram depicting God the Father → Christ → Husband → Wife. This diagram shows a chain of command or order of responsibility only—not levels of worth or importance. In the divine hierarchy, though the Father and Son have different roles, they are equal (John 10:30; 14:9). And in the husband-wife relationship, the question isn't who is superior or more privileged, but who is responsible for leadership in God's family organization.

3. Ask, *What are the strengths of living your family life based on this chain of command? What are the potential pitfalls or abuses?* See especially the section entitled "Deadbeat and Dictator."

4. Ask, *What does it mean to be the head of the household? What does it not mean? How do you think it should work in practice?*

5. The concept of the family as a complex organization, with the father as its president, has many practical implications for the man of the house. As a group, brainstorm a list of responsibilities of the president of a business organization. Write the list on your whiteboard or flip chart. (Responsibilities of a business executive include decision-making, delegation, goal-setting, evaluation of profits and products, and study to advance his knowledge of the business.)

6. Ask, *How are the responsibilities of a family head like these responsibilities of a business president? How does each of these responsibilities express itself in the life of a husband and father? In what ways is leading a family different from leading a business?*

7. Ask, *What responsibilities could be delegated to the wife? What types of decisions is the husband responsible for?*

8. Ask, *What types of goals should be set for the family?*

9. In Matthew 20:20–28, Jesus described two contrasting styles of leadership: dictatorial rule and servant leadership, which He modeled for His disciples. Have someone read this passage aloud. Then draw two columns on the board. Label one column "Servant Leadership" and the other "Dictatorial Leadership." The dictatorial approach to leadership is authoritarian, a "lord it over" system. Ask the group for examples of ways Jesus exemplified the servant approach. (For example, He washed the disciples' feet in John 13:4–5. He also gave up His life for those He led.) Ask, *What does servant leadership involve?* Write the group's answers in the first column. Jesus's comments in Matthew 20:20–28 can serve as a thought-starter.

10. Ask, *How does dictatorial leadership express itself?* Write answers in the second column. Invite answers about both actions and motives. Here are some possible answers:

DICTATORIAL LEADERSHIP	SERVANT LEADERSHIP
Sees responsibility as a job to perform, a necessary obligation	Sees responsibility as a ministry, as opportunity
Motivated by personal gain, earthly rewards	Motivated by personal gain, earthly rewards
"Do as I *say*" approach	"Do as I *do*" approach
Demands respect	*Earns* respect
Pulls rank, leads on basis of a designated position	Leads by example
Independent (doesn't easily accept suggestions)	Interdependent (willing to hear suggestions)
Superior attitude	Humble attitude
Aim is progress, to get ahead	Aim is transformation of self and others toward Christlikeness
Self-centered	Others-centered
Enjoys being served	Makes habit of serving others

11. Ask, *To which style of leadership will wives and children respond more positively? Why?* (The servant style. It is perceived as more personal, loving.)

12. Ask the group to discuss how each type of leader would respond to the following circumstances: (a) the need to establish rules governing his teenage daughter's social life; (b) how to spend a tax refund; (c) a child's deliberate act of disobedience, such as lying.

13. Ask, *Which one of the ten management policies at the end of the chapter would you most like to practice more effectively?*

14. Divide into subgroups of three or four. Ask each person to share with the other members of his subgroup a specific prayer request in response to the question "What changes do I need to make as head of my home?" One of the others can pray briefly for the need expressed before the next person shares.

ACTIVITIES BEFORE NEXT SESSION

Ask group members to do the following:

1. Read chapter 5 of the book.

2. Bring to the next session any Christian periodical, book, or resource that has helped you in the area of child raising or discipline in the home.

Session 5

TRAINER IN RESIDENCE

SESSION GOAL

To understand and apply what God's Word says about nurturing children.

PREPARATION

1. Study chapter 5.

2. Try to arrange for a tabletop display of Christian literature on the subject of child discipline and education in the home. Check your church library as well as friends. Have this display set up before the first group member arrives. Group members will add to the display the resources that have been most helpful to them.

3. Make photocopies of the worksheet "Training Principles from Proverbs" in Appendix A for each group member.

DISCUSSION

1. As group members arrive, encourage them to examine the literature display. If they bring books about nurturing children, ask them to add their books to the display and pick them up after the session.

2. As a warm-up to the discussion, ask, *What is one thing your parents did right in training you?* See if each person can come up with one thing, but allow people to pass or say nothing, if they prefer.

3. Write Proverbs 22:6 on a flip chart or board. Ask a few people to share their first thought—positive or negative—to this promise. *What questions come to your mind when you read this verse?*

4. If it's helpful, here is some background to the passage from Proverbs: In Israel at the time when the proverbs were composed, children were trained almost exclusively in the home by their parents. Training began at an early age and centered on understanding and applying the Law. Even before the giving of the Law, Abraham was obligated to instruct his whole household (Gen. 18:19). Every father was required to instruct his children (Ex. 10:2; 12:26–27). Passages that reflect the importance of transmitting God's truth from one generation to the next include Deuteronomy 6:1–9, Psalm 78:3–6, and Proverbs 4:3–4. The nature of instruction involved cultivating the child's memory to enable him to remember the Law. Parents also trained children in everyday duties (1 Sam. 16:11; 2 Kings 4:18), artistic abilities (1 Sam. 16:15–18; Ps. 137), and household skills (Ex. 35:25–26; Prov. 31:13–31). Mothers as well as fathers were important as trainers (Prov. 1:8; 6:20). Proverbs 31:1 indicates that Lemuel, the king of Massa, was taught by his mother. But training was ultimately the responsibility of the father in the Jewish system.

5. Ask, *Do you think it's more difficult to properly train a child now than when Proverbs 22:6 was written? Why or why not?*

6. Ask, *What accounts for the apparent discrepancy between the promise in Proverbs 22:6 and the lack of success of many Christian parents?* (Many different sources shape a child's value system today, and many parents misunderstand what is actually involved in the training process.)

7. Ask, *What are the most common problems you encounter in trying to train your children for Christ?* Write responses on a flip chart or board. Ask, *What insights or solutions have some of you discovered concerning any of these problems?*

8. Go over each of the steps the chapter gives for leading children in the way they should go. Ask questions like these:

Which of these steps do you find most challenging?

What is it about that step that is difficult for you?

Why is a negative influence easier for a child to pick up than a positive one?

How do you think a person goes about learning to communicate better with children?

How does a parent learn to handle frustration better?

What insights on training did you find most helpful in the chapter?

9. If you have time, distribute the photocopied worksheet on Proverbs. Give everyone about ten minutes to complete it. Then ask members of the group to share their conclusions. What follows are some possible gleanings from these references.

The motive for child discipline should be love (3:12). Discipline is proof of my love for my child (3:12). Discipline should be consistent and firm (13:24, note the term *diligent*). Extreme physical punishment that could injure a child must be avoided (19:18b). Discipline should begin early while the child is young (19:18, note the phrase *while there is hope*). Discipline can have a positive eternal effect that shapes the destiny of a child (23:14). We sin when we hold back discipline (23:13a). Discipline is needed because of the child's innate bent toward foolishness and sin (22:15). Results of discipline include wisdom in the child (29:15) and delight in the hearts of parents (29:17).

10. Divide into subgroups of three or four people for prayer. Ask each person to verbalize specific prayer requests related to the training of their children. After an individual shares a request, have another member of that subgroup who can identify with the need pray briefly for that individual. Also encourage members of each subgroup to pray for one another during the coming week.

ACTIVITIES BEFORE NEXT SESSION

Ask group members to read chapter 6. As leader, you should do this as well:

1. Study Ephesians 5:22–33.

2. Optional: briefly interview six or eight women whose families aren't represented in this course and record their responses to this incomplete sentence: "I feel most loved by my husband when _____." You may choose to delegate this task of interviewing to a group member. Try to get specific responses from the interviewees.

REAL LOVE

SESSION GOALS

1. To discover ways Christ loved the church and the implications for a husband-wife relationship.

2. To determine one way we can become more Christlike in our love for our wives.

PREPARATION

1. Study chapter 6.

2. Take pencils, writing paper, and 3 x 5 cards to the session.

3. See Activity 2 in session 5. If you chose to delegate this responsibility, call the interviewer to ask how he or she is doing. The interviewer should be prepared to share the interviews during the session.

4. You may also want to photocopy the outline of Ephesians 5:22–33 in Appendix B for group members. Paul's instructions to marriage partners are in a context that speaks of the believer's total walk with Christ (Eph. 4–6), pointing out that a man cannot truly walk with Christ unless his marriage and family life are in order. The repetition of references to the Lord in Ephesians 5:22–33 shows the centrality God wants to have in every marriage (twelve uses of Christ's name or of pronouns substituting for His name).

The command to love our wives (5:25) is the Greek present imperative tense and could be translated as "keep on loving" or "make a habit of loving." The word *sanctify* in verse 26 means "to set apart as holy, as for a special purpose." The phrase *having no spot* means "having no impurity," and the word *wrinkle* refers to any sign of decay or ruin. Repetition of the word *own* (twice in verse 28 and again in verse 33) reveals the Lord's insistence that we have only one woman as the object of our thoughts and affection. It suggests God's displeasure with lust and emotional attachment to other women.

DISCUSSION

1. Put the declaration "Love Is Never Free" on the whiteboard as a thought starter. Ask, *Do you agree or disagree with this statement? Why?* Allow several minutes for comments, then point out that the phrase *free love* is one of numerous statements that reflect a distorted or watered-down definition of the term. In this session, your group will explore misconceptions of love and learn what the husband-wife love relationship should be like. The author insists that all love costs somebody something. Ask your group to name some of the costs of real love.

2. Help group members understand that the way society uses the term *love* can be vastly different from the way Scripture uses it. Ask, *What are the common counterfeits of love—attitudes or feelings people often mistake for love?* (Some examples: yearning for glamour or adventure; sexual attraction; longing for a mother or father substitute; desire for status, appreciation, or social acceptance; and the need to depend on someone.)

3. Ask, *What are the basic differences between feelings and love?* (Feelings are often self-centered, causing a person to think in terms of what a relationship can do for him, whereas love focuses more on the other person's fulfillment. Feelings are also temporary; they

come and go. A commitment that permanently binds two people together reflects love. Love includes feelings but is based more on commitment than on emotion.)

4. Ask, *What accounts for so much confusion over the meaning of love?*

5. Have someone read Ephesians 5:22–33 aloud. You may want to give copies of the outline in Appendix B to the group or direct group members to the outline in their books.

6. Make two columns on the board, titling them "Ways Christ Loved the Church" and "Implications for Husbands." Ask, *What are some concrete ways in which Christ expressed love to the church?* Encourage the group to refer to the four gospels for illustrations of how Jesus loved the church or His followers.

For instance, Christ loved the church *sacrificially* (the cross); *unconditionally* (Rom. 5:6, 8); *unselfishly, consistently, verbally* (He told others He loved them—John 13:34; 15:12); *prayerfully* (John 17); *patiently* (note illustrations of patience with His disciples); *forgivingly* (Peter in John 21); *gently* (John 20, with Mary near the tomb); *tearfully* (compassion for Lazarus and family in John 11). The illustrations of Christ's love should show that He loved others both through *deeds* and *words* of comfort, encouragement, and praise.

7. Ask, *What are the implications for husbands of the concrete ways we just listed?* For example, one way Christ loved the church was to *initiate* love when it was undeserved (Rom. 5:6, 8; 1 John 4:9–10). One possible way for the husband to act as initiator of love is to be the first to apologize or make up after an argument—even if he feels the wife is 90 percent to blame for the quarrel. He needs to ask forgiveness for his 10 percent! A husband's love for his wife should be expressed in both *words* and *actions*. It's easy for men to take for granted a woman's need to hear that she's loved.

8. Ask, *What things often hinder the development of a love relationship between a husband and wife?* (The chapter points to some answers. For instance, a partner's poor self-image, his drive to excel in a job or hobby, or competitors such as television can become obstacles to closeness. Some of the obstacles listed may not be bad in themselves but can become preoccupations that drive a wedge between husband and wife.)

9. Play audio recordings of the interviews you had with women, or read aloud what the women said. The women's comments should reinforce and illustrate content written in the "Implications" column during the preceding activity. Hearing the tape can help make the men in the group sensitive to new ways in which they can express love to their wives.

10. If you didn't do the interviews and you have more time, you can look at 1 Corinthians 13. Love between husband and wife can be defined in two ways. There are *lexical* definitions that explain what the word means. For example, "Love is the capacity to understand my wife." Or, "Love is being kind to my wife." But an *operative*, or *behavioral* definition gives an even deeper understanding of love. A behavioral definition shows the word in action. For example, "Love is telling her I'm sorry when I've hurt her." Or, "Love is taking care of the kids while she goes to the gym." These are more concrete definitions that show love in action. First Corinthians 13 contains both types of definitions.

Ask someone to read 1 Corinthians 13:4–7 aloud. Then ask, *What are some things that love does?* For example, participants may say that love bears all things. Affirm this good answer and ask the group to put that into their own words. *What actions does bearing all things involve in a marriage?*

You can also ask, *What does love not do? What are important actions to avoid? What should we do instead?* For example, "Love does not consider a wrong suffered," means "love freely forgives the other person."

LOVE DEFINED NEGATIVELY	LOVE DEFINED POSITIVELY
Love is not jealous is not boastful is not arrogant is not unbecoming in behavior Love does not seek its own way does not focus on wrongs suffered is not easily provoked does not rejoice in unrighteousness	Love is patient is kind Love rejoices with the truth bears all things believes all things hopes all things endures all things

Next, ask the group to formulate questions that can help a man evaluate his marriage relationship in light of the characteristics in 1 Corinthians 13. For instance, "Love does not consider a wrong suffered." A searching question is, "Have I failed to forgive my wife for anything she has said or done?" Or, "Love is patient." A meaningful question is, "In what specific ways do I need to be more patient with my spouse?"

11. Give each group member a 3 x 5 card. Ask each person to complete this sentence after meditating on the interviews and what you wrote in the "Implications" column: "I can be more Christlike in loving my wife (or husband) next week by _____." Allow time for silent prayer, in which participants can ask God for the courage and ability to put their ideas into practice.

ACTIVITIES BEFORE NEXT SESSION

Ask group members to do the following:

1. Read chapter 7.

2. Read Ephesians 4:29 and James 3:1–12.

THE OPENHEARTED MAN

SESSION GOAL

To improve communication with our partners by applying biblical principles about the tongue to our own lives.

PREPARATION

1. Read chapter 7, and examine James 3:1–12 and Ephesians 4:29.

2. Provide paper and pens.

3. To gain a wider perspective on the Bible's teaching on the tongue, you can also use a concordance and look up references to *tongue, lips, mouth, words,* and *talk* in Proverbs. Look for positive and negative uses of speech.

DISCUSSION

1. Launch this session with the following question: *How many words do you think an average person speaks in a day?* (Many variables, such as one's personality and vocation, make it difficult to estimate. But a survey indicated that about twenty-five thousand to thirty thousand is average. Most guesses from your group will probably be lower.) After citing the suggested average, ask a volunteer to read Proverbs 10:19. This verse indicates that the more we talk, the more likely we are to make mistakes with our tongue.

2. Ask, *Think of someone you know who communicates well. What is one thing that person does that makes him or her an effective communicator?*

3. It's helpful to have concrete examples of both shallow and intimate husband-wife communication. Write two column headings on your whiteboard or flip chart: "Shallow" and "Intimate." Ask the group for specific illustrations of shallow communication within marriage. An example could be the husband's habit of reading his phone or texting during a shared meal.

4. Then ask for specific illustrations of intimate communication within marriage. An example is a man sharing prayer requests related to his job.

5. Give everyone a piece of paper and a pen. Ask someone to read Ephesians 4:29 aloud. Then ask everyone to come up with three questions he could use to evaluate his words and actions in a conversation with his wife. Allow two or three minutes of silence while group members write their questions. Finally, invite people to share their questions. (Examples of questions are: *Will what I'm about to say build up my spouse or tear her down? In what way could the words I'm about to say be destructive to her? What need will my words meet? Will what I say give grace to her?*)

6. Ask, *In what ways can husbands build up their wives through conversation?* (Greeting her warmly upon arriving home after work; complimenting her appearance or something she's done; asking her questions about her day; giving her constructive feedback rather than criticism.)

7. Ask, *When did another person say something that built you up or met a personal need?* Have members share what the other person said, how it made them feel, and why. After hearing several illustrations, stress that this is what we want our conversation to do for our wives.

8. Instruct group members to look at the hindrances to communication listed in the chapter. Ask, *Have there been times when you recognized any of these hindrances in your marriage? What was the impediment? How did God expose the need? How is He helping you overcome this obstacle, or how could He help you?*

9. Instruct group members to look at the helps to communication listed in the chapter. Ask, *What helps could be added to this list?* (Encourage answers based on the experience of group members.)

10. Ask, *How have you used one or more of these helps? How has God empowered you to do this?*

11. Ask, *Which help is most difficult for you to implement, and why?*

12. Ask, *Look at the five levels or circles of communication discussed in the chapter. Which level best describes your marriage? What do you need to do to progress to a deeper level? Which hindrances need removing? Which helps should you take the initiative to implement this week?*

13. Have group members get into subgroups of three or four people to pray for each other about their answers to question 12.

ACTIVITIES BEFORE NEXT SESSION

Read chapter 8.

Session 8

JESUS'S MAN

SESSION GOALS

1. To highlight what we've learned in this study.

2. For those who do not know Christ to accept Him as Savior.

3. For those who know Him to depend wholly on Him for the power to apply what we've learned in this study.

PREPARATION

1. Study chapter 8.

2. If you suspect that anyone in the group lacks a relationship with Christ as Lord and Savior, then it would be good at some point in this final session to talk about how to receive Christ. If you don't know how to go about this, your pastor may have suggestions. There are also simple approaches available online. For example, Dr. Stanley gives a short presentation of the gospel on the In Touch Ministries website at intouch.org/you/all-things-are-new. You may want to go over this during your meeting or get together with a group member one-on-one.

DISCUSSION

1. Ask, *How has this study affected you as a husband and/or father in the past month? What is one difference it has made?* Encourage as many men as possible to respond, but allow people to pass if they want to.

2. This is a related but not identical question. There's a crucial difference that goes to the theme of this session: what it means to be a spiritual man. Ask, *How has your faith in Christ affected you as a husband and/or father in the past month? What difference has Christ made?* Draw attention to the difference. Ask men if their answers are the same as above, or if they want to add something or say something different. If some group members aren't believers, it's fine for them to pass. The point here is for group members to discern whether Jesus—the living Person—is active in their lives or whether they're just gleaning tips on relationships that they could get from any good psychologist. Such tips are much better than nothing! But without Christ active in our lives, we'll inevitably have something missing as husbands and fathers. We can get only so far under our own steam.

3. If you want to share how to receive Christ, this is a good time to do so. Welcome questions and discussion. Give opportunity for response through silent prayer, and encourage anyone who made a decision to chat with you after the session.

4. The chapter suggests various ways a man can model his faith to his family: asking them to pray about something, praying with them, having nightly chats, having daily devotions and not hiding them from the family, taking the family to a good church, and so

on. Ask, *If you're already doing one or more of those things, talk about what you're doing. How do you think it is affecting your family?*

5. Ask, *What challenges do you face in consistently praying with and listening to your kids, or in having your own daily devotions?* Allow the group to problem solve and to come up with workable solutions. However, beware of anyone who is too free with advice for others and rarely talks about his own shortcomings. Do not allow this person to dominate the conversation. Encourage people to say, "This is what I do," rather than, "This is what you should do." And remind the group that letting a man talk about what he's dealing with is often far more helpful than trying to fix his problem.

In some cases, a man might not want to admit that he's afraid to pray with his family or ask them to pray about something. You can pose that hypothetically: *What if a guy has never prayed with his kids before bed and is nervous about starting? Where do you think he should begin?*

6. Ask, *Does anybody have any questions they want to discuss about any of the material in the book?* Discuss these as a group.

7. Divide into subgroups of three or four people. Ask each person to share (1) the most helpful insight he or she has gleaned from this study and (2) a prayer request in light of the shortcomings or needs exposed by the study. After each person shares, one or more members of the subgroup can pray for him or her before moving to the next person.

APPENDIX A

Training Principles from Proverbs

Beside each reference, summarize the verse in your own words. Study these passages; then in the "conclusions" section, list the significant observations or guiding principles you see.

Proverbs 3:12 _____

_____

Proverbs 13:24 _____

_____

Proverbs 19:18 _____

_____

Proverbs 22:15 _____

_____

Proverbs 23:13–14 _____

_____

Proverbs 29:15 _____

_____

Proverbs 29:17 _____

_____

CONCLUSIONS:

APPENDIX B
Ephesians 5:22-33 Outline

I. Instructions to Wives: Submit (vv. 22–24)

    A. To Your Own Husbands (v. 22)

    B. As to the Lord (v. 22)

    C. Rationale for Submission: Headship of Husband (v. 23)

    D. As Church Is Subject to Christ (v. 24)

    E. In Everything (v. 24)

II. Instructions to Husbands: Love (vv. 25–30)

    A. How to Love Your Wife

        1. As Christ Loved the Church (v. 25)

        2. As Christ Gave Himself for the Church (v. 25)

        3. As Your Own Bodies (v. 28)

        4. As You Nourish and Cherish Your Own Flesh (v. 29)

    B. Evidences of Loving Her

        1. Sanctifying Her (v. 26)

        2. Cleansing Her with Word (v. 26)

        3. Presenting Her (v. 27)

a. Without Spot

b. Without Wrinkle

c. Holy

d. Blameless

III. The Making of a Marriage (v. 31)

A. Leave Parents

B. Cleave to One Another

C. Become One Flesh

IV. Marriage Analogy: Christ and the Church (v. 32)

V. Summary of Paul's Instruction (v. 33)

A. To Husbands: Love

B. To Wives: Respect

NOTES

CHAPTER 2

1. "Young Adults and Liberals Struggle with Morality," The Barna Group, www.barna.org, August 25, 2008, http://www.barna.org/teens-next-gen-articles/25-young-adults-and-liberals-struggle-with-morality. Used with permission.

2. Gibson Winter, *Love and Confict: New Patterns in Family Life* (New York: Doubleday, 1958), 68.

3. Carl Sandburg, "Address of Carl Sandburg before the Joint Session of Congress," February 2, 1959, http://www.nps.gov/carl/historyculture/upload/Address-of-Carl-Sandburg-before-the-Joint-Session-of-Congress.pdf.

4. William Booth, quoted in Royal Gould Wilder, Delavan Leonard Pierson, Arthur Tappan Pierson, et al., *The Missionary Review of the World* (New York: Funk & Wagnalls Company, 1911), 796.

5. Edith Deen, *Great Women of the Christian Faith* (Westwood, NJ: Barbour, 1959), 222.

CHAPTER 5

1. Theodore Roosevelt, "The Duties of American Citizenship" (speech, 1883), http://www.pbs.org/wgbh/americanexperience/features/primary-resources/tr-citizen/.

CHAPTER 6

1. Edith Lindeman and Carl Stutz, "Little Things Mean a Lot," © 1954 Leo Feist, Inc. Used by permission.

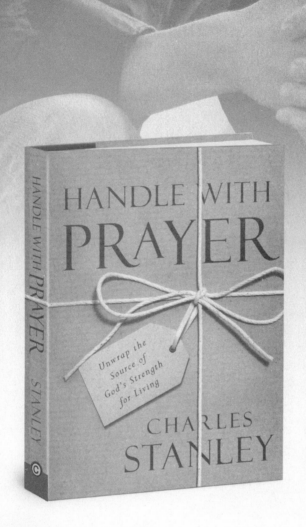

The best-selling guide to the
power of prayer

**A revised and refreshed take on Dr. Charles Stanley's landmark
bestseller.** How can we cultivate a prayer life that makes a difference?
Now enhanced with a study guide, this modern-day classic uncovers the
power found when we connect with God.